STREAMS OF LIVING WATER

STREAMS OF LIVING WATER

BY
MARTIN DOWN

STRUIK CHRISTIAN BOOKS

MONARCH
CROWBOROUGH

First British edition 1996

ISBN 1 85424 336 5

British Library Cataloguing in Publication Data.
A catalogue record for this book is available
from the British Library.

Co-published in South Africa with
Struik Christian Books Ltd.,
Cornelis Struik House, 80 McKenzie Street,
Cape Town 8001, South Africa.
Reg no 04/02203/06

Designed and produced in England for
MONARCH PUBLICATIONS
Broadway House, The Broadway,
Crowborough, East Sussex TN6 1HQ by
Nuprint Ltd, Harpenden, Herts AL5 4SE.

CONTENTS

This book is dedicated to
the people of St George's and St Nicholas'
whose story this is,
and to God
who has done it.

PREFACE

This book is about how the so-called 'Toronto Blessing' came to two small English country parishes.

The first thing that they tell you in Toronto is that Toronto cannot bless you: only God can bless you. So it is God's blessing, not the Toronto blessing. Yet the phrase 'Toronto Blessing' is a useful short-hand way of describing a new wave of the Holy Spirit's blessing which began in Toronto in January 1994. The story of that is told in other places, such as *Catch the Fire* by Guy Chevreau (Marshall Pickering 1994), and I am not attempting to cover that story again.

The earlier history of our two churches, St Nicholas' and St George's, will be familiar to those who have read *Speak to These Bones* (Monarch 1993). But I have tried not to assume that everyone has read these books first. I hope that *Streams of Living Water* stands by itself.

As before I have used the real names of the people who feature in this story. Where people are named, I have shown them the manuscript and obtained their permission before exposing them to print. I have occasionally simplified the narrative, but nothing has been invented. It is all as it happened. It is written, again, solely to encourage others and to give glory to God.

ONE

RIVERS OF DAMASCUS

'Why are you refusing to go to Toronto?'

It seemed as if the Lord was asking me a question. I was on my annual retreat, staying with the nuns. Various issues swam to the surface of my mind as I relaxed into the silence and peace of this spiritual oasis. One of them was Toronto.

Just before I left home for the retreat, someone had said to me, 'It won't happen here until you go to Toronto.' Somehow it had seemed prophetic.

So why was I refusing to go? My wife Maureen had been pestering me about going ever since we had begun to hear about the Toronto Blessing the previous summer. She wanted to go, and she wanted to go with me. But for some reason I was obstinately refusing to contemplate it.

It was not that I was against what I had seen and heard of this new move of the Holy Spirit. If anything, I was inclined to be blasé about it. There was very little that we had not seen or heard somewhere or other before. Anyone who had moved in charismatic Christian circles for long had seen people falling over, trembling, crying, occasionally laughing, as they were touched by the Spirit of God. So what was new?

There was undoubtedly a new intensity about the way that God was working now. At any one service or meeting many more people were being affected. There was a lot more laughter, not always confined to the times when the Holy Spirit was invited to come. There were more bizarre manifestations of the Spirit's power on people, jumping, bouncing, flailing arms and legs; more noise, even apparently animal noises like the roaring of lions.

But, together with all this, there were abundant stories of lives being changed, the ministries of pastors being revitalised (and pastors' wives), people coming into a new awareness of the love and power of God. I myself had received prayer by ministers who had experienced the Toronto Blessing in recent months. One difference from previous times of ministry was that I was 'slain in the Spirit'; I had felt myself pushed backwards, not by any human hand, for no one was even touching me, but by the hand of God. As I had lain on the floor it was not hilarious laughter that came up from my stomach but a contented chuckle.

Back home at our monthly celebrations on a Saturday night we continued, as we had done before, to invite God to come and minister to people according to their needs. We prayed with people and laid hands on them, and saw what, for us, were the usual sort of results. It was not nothing: God continued to come and bless and heal. But we were not seeing the sort of increase in the intensity of God's activity that we had been taught to expect from the Toronto Blessing.

All the time I refused to go to Toronto.

'Everyone who has been,' I protested, 'says that the blessing is transferable. You don't have to go to Toronto to get it. God knows our address. If he wants to send it, he'll send it.'

It did stick in my mind that someone had also said that some people from the parish *should* go; perhaps even, some of us in leadership *needed* to go. But I did not see the need, so I stubbornly resisted Maureen's importunity.

Now it seemed to be God who was getting at me. 'Why are you refusing to go to Toronto then?' I had my own agenda for this retreat, but God wouldn't let me ignore the question. Why was I?

It was, I saw, a sort of snobbery. For some reason that I could not explain, I had always resisted doing what everyone else was doing. As my children often remarked, I had never been a dedicated follower of fashion, which means I have always looked conservative and old-fashioned. If all the world was reading a particular novel, that was a very good reason for me not to read it. For years and years I had missed the pleasure of reading, for instance, *Doctor Zhivago*, for just that reason. If all the world was going to the Dordogne on holiday, then that was the last place on earth I wanted to go. It was only in the past two or three years that I had discovered for myself that the Dordogne was indeed one of the loveliest places on earth.

Now everybody was flying off to Toronto. So I was not going to go.

'So,' the Lord continued, 'I suppose that means, that if all the world was going out into the wilderness to be baptised by John in the river Jordan, you would not go.'

I felt a bit sheepish at this point, realising what a foolish and probably sinful attitude this was. After all, what would I have missed if I had refused to go out with everyone else to see John the Baptist? I would have simply missed out on what God was doing then. But I had to confess to Jesus, 'Yes, I suppose you're right. I would not have gone.'

'But I went,' he replied.

That did me altogether. Not only might I have missed out on what God was doing, but it was clear that Jesus did not share my fastidious attitude to crowds. What they were doing, he was happy to do. If everybody was getting baptised in the river Jordan, then he would too. He identified with the herd, whereas I wanted to dissociate myself from it.

I was a snob and Jesus was not. I was proud and Jesus was humble. I wanted to be different and Jesus was content to be the same. I was convicted of much more than my refusal to go to Toronto.

'But, I still don't see why,' I persisted. 'They all say that the blessing is transferable. They all say you don't have to go to Toronto; it can happen anywhere.'

'That's what Naaman the Syrian said,' the Lord replied.

That great man had taken offence at the word of the prophet Elisha. Having sought out the prophet in Israel to cure his leprosy, Elisha had told him, 'Go, wash yourself seven times in the Jordan, and your flesh will be restored, and you will be cleansed' (2 Kings 5:10). But Naaman objected, 'Why do I have to go to the Jordan to wash? What is wrong with the rivers at home?'

Here was I caught in the same sort of trap. No doubt, chemically speaking, there was no difference between the waters of the river Jordan and the waters of Abana and Pharpa, the rivers of Damascus. It was a matter of obedience. God had said, 'Wash in the Jordan'. So it was in the Jordan Naaman had to wash. There was no reasoning or bargaining about it. It was a word to be obeyed in meekness and humility. Likewise, there probably was no difference, chemically speaking, between the carpets of Toronto and the carpets of our own churches. But if the

Lord said, 'Go and lie on the carpet in Toronto,' to Toronto I had to go.

Finally, at my last gasp, I said, 'But it is terribly expensive'. Air fares, hotel bills, taxi-cabs loomed up before me.

'You've got the money in your Halifax,' the Lord replied.

I always thought bank accounts were supposed to be private, but here was God revealing to me that he had hacked into the computer at my Building Society. He was right, of course. 'But I'm saving up in that account to replace the car!' I wailed.

At which point the line went dead. The Lord had said all that he had to say. The rest was up to me.

When I returned from retreat a few days later, I picked up the phone and booked two flights to Toronto, one for Maureen – and one for me.

TWO
—

OUR FATHERS HAVE TOLD US

A village has a personality of its own. In a strange way each village has a sort of corporate character which is unique to itself, and which seems to endure even though individuals and whole generations of villagers come and go. Thus one village differs from another in character, as much as one person from another. Some of the differences can be explained in terms of the environment, both natural and built; others in terms of social arrangements and relationships. But there remains a factor which can only, I believe, be explained in spiritual terms.

There do seem to be spirits attached to places, perhaps what Paul meant by 'principalities and powers' or 'rulers and authorities' (Eph 6:12). The spirit of the place may seem benign: the village may seem friendly and accepting. Or the spirit of the place may be evil: one village can be a hotbed of gossip, another a cauldron of quarrels, another a sink of sexual iniquity. Unfortunately for the unwary newcomer, estate agents' brochures rarely tell you this when they advertise the property.

I am sure that the spirit of a place can be changed, in time. It is, I believe, the result of the history of the place, of the lives that have been lived there, and the habits that have been formed there, the things that have happened there. Somehow the accumulated influence of all this is passed on from one generation to another and it forms the character of the place. If the Spirit of God is breathed into the place, through prayer and Christian lives, it will be transformed. But change is slow.

Having been in rural ministry for fifteen years already, I had moved some six years previously to become rector of two new country parishes. In those six years a great deal had happened and much had changed, in the churches of St Nicholas' and St George's at least. Recognising the individuality of villages, I had not come expecting them to be the same. The two congregations were different, the traditions in their churches were different, and the churches had a different relationship with the villages at large. The pace of change in each church had been different, and they had travelled by different roads. But change there had certainly been in both places.

We had also felt the effect of changes in the Church of England as a whole. The rapid collapse of central funding had made demands on our local church finances which had never been made before. The continued reduction in the number of stipendiary clergy which the Church of England could afford to deploy brought the waves of pastoral reorganisation lapping once more around our shores. This time however we were not affected directly: the two parishes which had been joined together for pastoral purposes in my predecessor's time were left undisturbed. But uncertainty surrounded us.

More significant changes had come from our rediscovery of the power of the Holy Spirit, both in the life of the individual believer and in the life of the church. I had only made this discovery for myself in middle-age and mid-career, but it had radically changed me and the nature of my ministry. Coming to these two villages six years before, I had from the beginning shared this discovery with the people, and we had witnessed God changing lives and renewing the churches.

Change had not been without cost or pain, either for me, for others, or for the churches. Some people had left us, preferring to worship in other ways elsewhere. Both congregations had experienced splits, more or less openly: the main body had embraced the renewal and moved forward, but a minority in each church had retreated to the fringes where we still provided for people in more traditional ways. Since all rural Anglican churches are now organised in groups, the role of the parson has come to resemble that of the juggler: he has to keep several balls in the air at the same time. In my case it was only two, but even that had doubled the complications of leading a traditional church into renewal.

All the time we had seen a steady trickle of people coming into a new relationship with God through Jesus Christ. I would like to have seen a flood of such conversions, but God gave us at least a steady trickle. Again, we had seen a steady trickle of people being healed by the power of God. We had seen marriages and other relationships restored and made whole. There had always been something for which to praise God. Life had never been dull in those six years: we had seen God at work, and there is nothing more exciting in all the world than seeing God at work.

Yet even then we were looking for something more. As the psalmist said 'We have heard with our ears, O God, our fathers have told us what you did in their days, in days long ago' (Ps 44:1). We had heard of revivals in the past.

There were still Methodist chapels in each of our villages, sad and reproachful reminders of what God had done in days long ago. In the time of Wesley the Spirit of God had moved mightily through the land, even through the country villages, sweeping thousands of people into the Kingdom and establishing standards of holiness which had changed the life of the nation. In our generation we had not yet seen anything like that. Many of us were longing and praying for more: more than the renewal of the church – the revival of the nation.

The wind of the Spirit had certainly begun to blow through our churches. It had not been universally welcome. It had flicked over the pages of the old prayer books. It had raised dust and knocked over cherished objects. It had blown away air that had grown stale, and brought a new freshness into buildings which had become musty. But still, it was not that 'violent wind', that hurricane, which we read about on the day of Pentecost (Acts 2:2). Where was the Lord God of Elijah? the Lord God of the Apostles? The Lord God of Wesley and Whitfield? The Lord was adding to our number those who were being saved; year by year we could see it, but not yet day by day.

We believed and taught that Christians should be filled with the Holy Spirit, and we had seen God move in wonderful ways. We believed and taught that Spirit-filled Christians should use the gifts which the Spirit gives, and we had received significant words of wisdom, knowledge and prophecy. We believed and taught that people should lay hands on one another and pray for one another to be helped or healed, and God had honoured those prayers time and again. The trouble with all this is that it is addictive: the result of getting some is wanting more. The result of seeing some people healed is that you want to see more people healed. What about those who are apparently not healed? The result of receiving one revealing word is that you want to receive more. What about all those problems that remain obstinately unresolved? The result of seeing one person converted, coming from emptiness and despair to joy and purpose in the Lord, is that you want to see more. What about all those who are still without hope and without God in the world?

Human beings are made for addiction. The only problem is that they too easily become addicted to the wrong things, to things which are deceitful and harmful and destructive. We are meant to be addicted to God. After six years many of us were.

In six years St Nicholas' and St George's had changed from traditional Anglican churches, to churches that were openly and confidently charismatic, open to the Spirit of God and confident of his power to save. Not just that, they had become churches that were thirsty for more of God. So when God sent the next wave of the Holy Spirit over the church, the Toronto Blessing, we were ready for it.

Or were we?

THREE

—

WHENEVER THE CLOUD
LIFTED...

We were so constrained by time on a Sunday morning.

This issue also swam to the surface of my mind during my four-day retreat. It was an issue I had been meaning to address for some while. But amidst all the day-to-day business the strategic issues were constantly crowded out.

For six years I had operated a schedule which committed me to two main Sunday morning services, one at 9.30am at St George's, the second at 11.00am at St Nicholas'. This had never been really satisfactory. But what was the alternative?

Both villages were about the same size, so I had no reason to favour one rather than the other. I did not believe in any régime which required a calendar and a computer for people to work out when and where they should go to church. Habit is a great help in the Christian life, and people could not form habits if service times kept jumping about all over the place. So for six years this had seemed to be the best we could do.

However, I had always hoped to reach a point where it

was not necessary for me to leap into my car at the end of one service and leap out again two miles away just in time to start the next. In the eighteenth century there had been poorly-paid curates who had depended for a living on conducting as many services as possible every Sunday. They were known as 'gallopers', for at the end of each service they mounted a horse and galloped away to the next. I had been a galloper long enough. It was good neither for me nor for the congregations.

Both churches were constrained by time. The constraint was worse at St George's: everything we did as a church together had to be crammed into just over an hour, or I would be late at St Nicholas'. It was not a lot better at St Nicholas', with the knowledge that some people at least would be fidgeting if the main service went on much after twelve noon. There was lunch to get, and grandma to visit, and perhaps a non-Christian spouse waiting at home.

For several years we had offered people the opportunity for prayer and personal ministry after the services if they felt any need. We had a Ministry Team in both parishes whose members had some training and authority from me to pray with people in the church's name. Most Sundays a few people would avail themselves of this ministry, seeking help from God with personal problems or healing, as the case might be. But we usually had more hands available than heads to lay them on. Meanwhile the vast majority of the congregation in both churches would drink their coffee and go home.

For God to work as he was doing in Toronto we had to be able to offer a more general ministry of the Holy Spirit, and that meant more time than we seemed to have available in either church. The Toronto Blessing cannot be rushed. The essence of it is to wait upon God, to soak in the Holy Spirit. That requires time as much as anything else, and time seemed to be one thing we did not have. Was there any alternative?

Some two years before, Stephen and Pippa and their son Simon had come to St George's. Stephen was already part of the way through an extra-mural course of theological and pastoral studies, and he was hoping to follow this through and qualify as a Reader in the Church of England.

Since coming to us Stephen had finished his course, been accepted for Readership, and now for the last six months had held the bishop's licence to preach and teach. Not being ordained, he could not preside at the sacraments, but we could now use him as an alternative leader. I began to work out the possibilities and implications of such a change.

It would be possible to synchronise the main morning services, starting both at the same time, say 10.00am. Stephen could lead one, which would be a service of the Word, while I could lead the other, which could be a service of both Word and Sacrament. I could provide extra services of Holy Communion earlier in the morning for those who, like me, set a high value on the sacraments.

There would be snags. The chief one would be pastoral: my contact with the main body of worshippers would be a fortnightly one in both parishes, instead of a weekly one. It would be difficult for either Stephen or me to keep in touch with people and their on-going needs. This is a weakness built into any system which gives one pastor the care and responsibility of more than one church. That's the sort of ministry which many denominations demand of their ministers today, but it is not right. The church is the body of Christ, and each local church is meant to be the local manifestation of that body. A body, as Paul remarks, is made up of many parts (1 Cor 12:12). If Siamese twins are born sharing limbs or vital organs of any sort they do not tend to have much of a life expectancy. But we regularly ask churches to survive on shared leadership, especially in the countryside.

I had always had the long-term aim of developing new 'limbs and organs' in both these churches, to the point at which each church might have a complete set. Stephen coming to live in the parish of St George's, while I lived in the parish of St Nicholas', was a step in that direction. He was at least some sort of resident leadership for St George's. But so far this was only a step on the way. For the time being we were still in the situation of sharing vital functions between the two churches, and we had to find out how to make the best of it.

In the following months I discussed these issues with Stephen, with the Church Councils and with others, and we decided to introduce the necessary changes. My six years in these two parishes seemed to have been an almost continuous process of change, and here was yet another. Some people had reservations about it, but in this case the advantages were plain enough and we agreed to do it. I guess that many people, including me, sighed for the day when we could settle down and enjoy a period of stability and continuity. But that still lay in the future. The pillar of cloud and fire was moving on again and we had to move with it (Num 9:17). The Promised Land was ahead not behind; what lay behind was only Egypt, to which there was now no going back. Having started out on this journey with God, we had to keep moving on if we were to keep up with what he was doing. It seemed to be time to pack up our tents again.

Whatever we might be losing, we would be gaining time: time on a Sunday morning to let God be God.

FOUR

THE FLOODGATES WERE OPENED

For eighteen months we had been running the Alpha course. Alpha is a basic introduction to the Christian faith, a course developed over a number of years in a well-known West London church, Holy Trinity, Brompton. When we first heard about Alpha we recognised that it filled a real gap in our church programme.

Alpha would lay the foundations of the Christian life, or at least make sure of the foundations that had been laid. It was meant both for outsiders and for existing members of the church. It combined some good solid chunks of teaching with the opportunity for people to ask questions and explore their own difficulties. It was essentially a rolling programme that, once started, would fulfil an ongoing need in the life of our two churches.

Most older churches tend to take too much for granted. People have been coming to church for many years, maybe all their lives, and we tend to take it for granted that they have a personal relationship with the Lord. Someone new starts coming to church and we tend to take it for granted that they know about Jesus and what he did for them on the cross. Someone is firmly committed to the Christian faith and attends all the church meetings in sight, and we tend to take it for granted that they have a personal life of prayer and devotion. In fact none of these things can be taken for granted. It does not do anyone any harm to go back to basics for a few weeks and have the essentials brought into focus. This is what Alpha does for church-goers.

The renewal of the church always depends on personal renewal. The renewal of a church is certainly more than the renewal of individual members, but there is no renewal of the church without that. I had certainly never taken it for granted that everyone in the church had received the baptism of the Holy Spirit, indeed rather the opposite. But while most of the people in our two parishes, who had been part of the renewal of the church over the previous six years had been baptised in the Spirit, we needed a mechanism for ensuring that those who joined us subsequently would also enter into this blessing. Alpha does this too.

We were also looking out for new methods of evangelism. We had knocked on doors and had had most of them shut in our faces. Even where the front door of the house was opened to us there was another inner door to the heart which was usually kept firmly shut. We had invited our friends and neighbours to church for special events and for guest services. None of these efforts had been entirely fruitless, but we were acutely aware of the limitations of our methods.

Ordinary neighbourly contacts, either at home or at work, rarely give the opportunity for a sustained conversation or systematic presentation of the Christian faith. Bringing people to church does not give them any chance to talk about their own questions or concerns. It is difficult enough in any case to establish enough confidence with people to talk with them about things that really matter. The weather, the children, and our ailments are the stock-in-trade of ordinary conversation, not repentance, the person of Christ, or the work of the Holy Spirit.

Alpha provides an environment for all these needs to be met: for a sustained advocacy of the gospel, for people to respond and talk about their own difficulties, and for the cultivation of a fellowship in which people feel sufficient acceptance and security to open up their hearts and lives to one another.

So we had taken Alpha into our system. We hired the school hall, and one evening a week and one weekend a term was devoted to Alpha. The Lord blessed the course in our parishes, as he had done in many other places. Each term we had had about seventy people on the course. Of these, about twenty-five were helpers and group-leaders. To begin with, the course was largely made up of people from our own two congregations. As time went on we had an increasing number of people coming from other towns and villages and other churches. We found that some people were travelling up to twenty-five miles to come to our Alpha course.

Ian and Gill had moved in to one of our own villages, and Gill had started to come to St George's from the time they arrived. We suggested that Alpha would help her to make new friends, and also to find out where we were coming from as a church. Now in her forties, Gill had been a Christian for about ten years. Severe depression had followed a hysterectomy. Ian and Gill had been unable to have any children; and the final removal of her womb had left Gill feeling empty and useless. In other ways too she had taken some hard knocks in life, and she felt bitter and frustrated.

She had found help in a Christian house fellowship, and in the midst of her depression had prayed a prayer of repentance and faith and asked to be filled with the Holy Spirit. There had not been any dramatic changes in her life but she had started to go to church regularly, and when Ian had got a new job after leaving the Army, Gill at last believed that God might be on her side after all.

Another job change in which they could see the hand of God brought Ian and Gill to one of our villages. Even now Gill's faith was more a matter of the will than the heart, but that began to change during Alpha. When the course reached that bit of teaching she asked again to be filled with the Holy Spirit and God softened her heart for the first time. The accumulated resentment of the years began to dissolve and she found that she knew Jesus as a personal friend as never before.

Ian recognised that something had happened to Gill: the old bitterness was gone; she was more positive and light-hearted. Ian himself had been in the Army most of his life. At the age of twenty-one he had sustained a blow to the back of his head in an armoured car. Although the immediate effects did not seem to be too serious, a few weeks later a blood-vessel burst, flooding his brain with blood. He was rushed to hospital, his life in the balance. He recovered, but an area of his brain had been damaged, and he was left with distressing handicaps. Loss of memory was one of the least; more difficult were a chronic lack of self-confidence, and sudden and inexplicable changes of mood. From cheery good-humour, he would abruptly plunge into cynicism and despair. Not only his wife but his fellow soldiers found him difficult to handle. Years of consultations with neurologists and psychiatrists had failed to achieve any improvement. The Army had kept him on light duties, but his mental state prevented him from gaining any further promotion.

All through these years Ian had retained a basic faith in God, but his faith was a bit like his career, mostly in a state of suspended animation. However when Gill suggested that he might like to attend the next Alpha course he readily agreed. Ian came with a serious intention. There had to be more to life than this, he said to himself. He thought carefully about what he heard. He prayed a prayer asking for the forgiveness of his sins. He asked Jesus to come into his life. Finally he asked God to fill him with the Holy Spirit.

Before he knew where he was, he was flat on his face on the floor, with Gill incredulous beside him. Then laughter began to bubble up inside, and finally it burst out. Roaring with laughter as he lay on the ground Ian was somehow healed of all his traumas. He had neither laughed nor cried, nor felt nor expressed any real emotion for thirty years. That day a sort of Noah's flood ended Ian's drought: 'on that day all the springs of the great deep burst forth and the flood gates of the heavens were opened' (Gen 7:11). A new man arose from the floor, confident of himself, with a new temperament, a cheerful and happy demeanour, a new outlook on life and a new song in his heart.

The laughing in the Spirit returned again and again over the following weeks and Ian discovered that he had an intimate relationship with God that he had never known before. Gill found it hard at times to cope with her new man. One evening as the Spirit came upon him, he quietly left the room where they were watching television. Going to look for him some time later, Gill found him sitting by himself in the other room, laughing.

'Are you all right?' she said.

'Yes,' Ian replied. 'Go away, I'm with the Lord.'

And Gill went away marvelling – and just a teeny bit envious.

FIVE

THE MINISTRY OF THE SPIRIT

D-Day for the new régime on Sundays was fixed for March 12th. Released from the old constraints of time, we could introduce into the services several elements which people had asked for: a return to the recitation of the psalms and testimonies of how God was working in the lives of members of the congregation. Above all, we would also have time to let the Holy Spirit move during the Sunday morning service.

Stephen and I had discussed at some length how to integrate the ministry of the Holy Spirit with the rest of the service. It seemed to us that it had to follow the ministry of the Word. That entailed a certain amount of re-arrangement of the order of service, for the sermon had not usually come at the end. And it seemed to pose an insuperable problem when it came to a Communion service. There, the sermon had to come in the middle and could not possibly come at the end. However we made some provisional adjustments which would, we hoped, enable a ministry of the Holy Spirit to follow the ministry of the Word.

This was the pattern that we had seen and experienced elsewhere, and there also seemed to be a certain spiritual

dynamic which demanded it. In 2 Corinthians 3 Paul contrasts two covenants or dispensations or ministries: the
ministry of the letter or the written code, and the ministry
of the Spirit. This whole chapter repays careful study as a
basis for the ministry of the Spirit. The distinction there
is clearly that between the Old Testament and the New,
between the dispensation of Moses and the dispensation
of Christ. But the exact points of difference need to be
noticed.

On the one hand, the old covenant depends upon letters, the letters of the law; on the other hand, the new
covenant depends on the Spirit. In the first the letters are
written either on tablets of stone or with ink on paper (it
does not matter which); in the second ministry, the Holy
Spirit writes, as it were, a letter from Christ on human
hearts. The difference lies in where the letters are written
and by what means.

Too often in the church we have misunderstood the
contrast. We have taken the difference between the two
dispensations to lie in the letters: the old dispensation to
be that of the letters of the law, the new dispensation to be
that of the letters of the gospel. Too often then, we have
ended up simply exchanging one set of letters on a page
for another: the old law of the Ten Commandments has
simply been replaced by a new law of the two great commandments. Instead of being Jews exercised about the
tithing of herbs or the observance of the sabbath, we have
become Christians exercised about whether we are loving enough or joyful enough.

Of course there is a difference in the message: the
basis of our relationship to God has changed. Under the
old covenant a right relationship with God depended on
what we did ourselves; under the new covenant it
depends on what Jesus has done for us. But even this

change can be misunderstood. The salvation which Jesus has won for us has to be claimed or appropriated by faith. Even this can be understood as a new law. Instead of being anxious about ritual cleanness, as of old, we are now anxious about whether we have enough faith. If this is the way the new covenant is understood, any doubts lead to a paroxysm of guilt, and any questioning to a panic of insecurity.

But that is not the point of the contrast. The difference between the old covenant and the new does not lie only in the message or the letters: no less importantly it lies in where that message is written, and by what or by whom it is written. This contrast is brought out even in the Old Testament:

> 'The time is coming,' declares the Lord, 'when I will make a new covenant with the house of Israel and with the house of Judah. It will not be like the covenant I made with their forefathers when I took them by the hand to lead them out of Egypt, because they broke my covenant, though I was a husband to them,' declares the Lord. 'This is the covenant that I will make with the house of Israel after that time,' declares the Lord. 'I will put my law in their minds and write it on their hearts. I will be their God, and they will be my people' (Jer 31:31-33).

The contrast lies in the *place* where the law is written: in the old covenant in letters on stone, in the new on human hearts and minds.

Likewise the Old Testament contrasts the writing instruments:

> I will give you a new heart and put a new spirit in you; I will remove from you your heart of stone and give you a heart of flesh. And I will put my Spirit in you and

move you to follow my decrees and be careful to keep my laws (Ezek 36:26-27).

The new work that God will do in the heart will be done by new *means*: no more with ink, but now by the Spirit.

The dynamic therefore of what Paul himself calls 'the ministry of the Spirit' (2 Cor 3:8) is that we speak the Word and the Holy Spirit writes it on our hearts. This can of course be an instantaneous process; as we speak, it is done. On the other hand we can too easily short-circuit the process, take the ministry of the Holy Spirit for granted, and give neither space nor weight to his part of the work. One of the discoveries of the contemporary renewal is simply that the more time the Holy Spirit is given, the more he will do. The ministry of the Word needs to be followed by the ministry of the Spirit.

However, it seems equally clear that this ministry of the Spirit needs to be preceded by a serious ministry of the Word. Exposition of the Word of God can alone give meaning and purpose to the ministry of the Holy Spirit. Without that, whatever might happen afterwards is in danger of degenerating into self-indulgence or something worse. So, we decided to tie together the ministries of the Word and the Spirit.

On March 12th we began to do it. We preached the Word, Stephen in one church and I in the other, then we asked everyone to stand, and we invited the Holy Spirit to come. After a little while we suggested people might step out into the aisles where the prayer-ministry team could lay hands on them.

The results did not seem to Stephen and me to be all that dramatic. Most people who stepped out for prayer sank down as they were prayed for under the power of the Spirit. One woman started laughing hilariously – lovely, free, uninhibited laughter. One or two men collapsed in the pews without being touched. One or two people started to shake visibly, one or two to weep. After a time we said a blessing, gave permission for people to leave, or to stay for more prayer and ministry if they wished.

Compared to what we had seen and heard elsewhere the manifestations of the Holy Spirit did not seem to be that sensational. But the reaction to it all, over the next few weeks, was. The whole church seemed to blow up.

Over the following days, I received phone calls and letters; people arrived on the doorstep and stopped me in the street. Some were furious; some were disturbed; some were worried for themselves; other were worried on behalf of others. Some left the church on the spot; some had a crisis of faith; some were frightened. Other people were grieving over the damage that seemed to have been done, the labours of love that seemed to have been lost.

I could not quite make out what had happened. Most of the people who were coming to these two services had been filled with the Spirit (most, though not all). Most of the people in the two congregations had been through the Alpha course. There they had learned something about the work of the Holy Spirit, and had had first hand experience of it on at least two occasions, going on around them if not touching them personally. What was the big deal now?

There were days then when I felt as though I was surveying the wreckage of some great air disaster. I had thought that we were simply taking on board an extra piece of luggage. But this piece of luggage had turned out to be a bomb which had blown the plane out of the sky. As I wandered about the scene of the crash I kept, as it were, coming across dead bodies, and met other survivors, in an equally dazed state, muttering vaguely to one another, 'What happened to us?'

As the smoke cleared it became evident that there were more survivors than at first appeared likely. People began helping each other up and applying first aid to the walking wounded. After a few weeks we could realistically start estimating the losses, and we began inquiring into the nature of the explosion. It was to take months to put the pieces back together again. When we did, it was a significantly different plane and crew that took to the air.

SIX

THEY PARTED COMPANY

One of the chief casualties was the leader of the music group at St Nicholas'. His resignation came as a devastating blow to the congregation.

In fact it was not as sudden as it appeared. For several months I had been spending time with this key person talking over a variety of issues which troubled him. He had been deeply unhappy at the decision of the Church of England to ordain women. Although this had not yet had any direct impact in our two parishes, we did have one or two women in the congregation who were candidates for ministry and the churches as a whole were willing to support them. Our worship-leader, on the other hand, believed that the subordination of women to men, clearly taught in Scripture in the context of marriage and the home, was of such a universal application that it precluded a woman being in any position of authority over men. He believed that the explicit words of Paul about the position and behaviour of women in the church, in the first letter to Corinth (1 Cor 11:3-16 and 14:34-35) and to Timothy (1 Tim 2:11-15), confirmed this view.

I myself had always found the question difficult to resolve. These Pauline passages about the position of women in the church are heavily obscure, and at their plainest it is not clear whether Paul is enunciating an eternal and universal principle or merely expressing his own opinion and making rules for his own situation. In scriptural interpretation I am guided by the axiom that what is important is clear and what is not clear is not important. In the end it did not seem to matter, even to Paul, by whom the gospel was preached, so long as somehow the gospel was preached (Phil 1:15-18). I therefore could accept the decision which the Church of England had made. The leader of our music group could not.

There were other issues involved as well, if anything deeper ones, and more closely related to the ministry of the Holy Spirit. These issues came to a head over the choice of songs we should sing, but underneath were questions of how the Holy Spirit works. The leader of the music group was not happy with songs which called upon God to act: 'Send Your Spirit', 'Draw me closer', 'Light the fire again'. He believed that we should emphasise the things that God had already done for us, both historically in the life, death and resurrection of Jesus Christ, and in our own personal lives, when he had called us and filled us with the Holy Spirit. After that, he believed that the emphasis needed to be on our responsibility, to go and share the gospel with others, to do the things that Jesus had done, to heal the sick and drive out demons, and to make our own lives holy and pleasing to God. For Spirit-filled Christians to say 'Come, Holy Spirit,' again and again, was unnecessary, unscriptural, and unhelpful.

Many hours we spent talking about this, and many hours I spent thinking about it. In a curious way it seemed to boil down to a matter of spiritual geography. Where was the Holy Spirit located? Certainly for Spirit-filled Christians, he was within them (Jn 14:17). But did that mean that he was not also outside them? Moreover, the Holy Spirit, wherever he was, was not passive or static, but was someone who moved and acted. Being within Christians, he certainly moved and acted both in them and through them. But did that mean that he did not move and act outside them also? If he moved outside them, then why not ask him to come to them, even again and again?

We all need pictures or stories to help us to understand spiritual things. Very few people can operate only with abstract concepts. That is why God has revealed himself in history and why Jesus taught in parables. Most of the pictures which the Scriptures give us of the Holy Spirit are elemental and dynamic: wind, fire and water. When the Bible gives us different pictures of the same thing they may not always be reconcilable with one another. The manifestation of the Holy Spirit as a dove alighting and remaining on Jesus is different from the manifestation of the Holy Spirit as a hurricane blowing through the room on the day of Pentecost. We need both pictures. Trying to picture how the Holy Spirit can be both within us and around us I could not do better for myself than think of a bottle in a river. The Holy Spirit may be compared to a river (Ezek 47:1-12), the river of God. I am like a bottle. At first I am outside the river and empty. Then, as I am baptised in the Holy Spirit, I am immersed in the river and the water flows in to fill me. Then the water is both inside and outside me; and the river moves and flows both inside and outside me.

Such an understanding of the Holy Spirit is no doubt paradoxical. But then much of Christianity is paradoxical: it is paradoxical that God is One and God is Three. It is paradoxical that God by his Spirit is both inside and outside us. But that is what the Scripture says, 'I will live in them and move among them' (2 Cor 6:16 RSV). That is exactly what we are asking God to do when we say, 'Come, Holy Spirit': we are asking the God who lives in us to move among us as well.

And he does. The simple fact is that when we ask in faith and expectation for the Holy Spirit to come and move among us, things happen. Superficial things happen; people fall over or tremble or shake; they laugh or cry or jump about. More profound things happen; people meet with God, see visions, hear God speaking; they are healed, set free from addictions, find peace of heart and mind. I found many of the theological issues that I discussed with our worship-leader difficult to clarify and resolve. But however imperfect my theological understanding of these things might be, I knew that I could not go back to a style or practice of ministry where everything depended on me. I had seen God working too often, using my faith and spiritual gifts on some occasions, on other occasions making up for what was lacking in my faith and spiritual gifts, but always doing more than I could ask or think. I could not close the door on this sort of ministry. It was something I was now committed to, long past the point of no return.

So once more we came to a place in the life of our churches which we had visited before. The particular issues might be different but the ultimate question was the same, 'Who was the leader here?' There always is a leader, or a group of leaders in the church. It is either the properly appointed leaders who are doing the leading, or it is someone else who is leading from the back seat or behind the scenes. Those appointed to lead need the courage of their convictions to lead on, even in the face of disagreement or disaffection. So I had to insist that we sing the songs, 'Send Your Spirit', 'Draw me closer', 'Light the fire again'. The leader of the music group resigned.

We did not quarrel. We both recognised the need for a leader to lead: he just could not follow my leadership any more in good conscience. There may indeed be times when the godly course is to part company without animosity. When Paul and Barnabas could not agree over taking Mark with them on their second journey, they simply parted company and went their separate ways (Acts 15:36-40). It does not seem to be the ideal solution, but in that case at least it had a happy ending. Years later we find Paul affirming the value of Mark (2 Tim 4:11). It seems as if, as so often, Barnabas was right, and that Mark eventually proved his worth even to Paul.

Such separations are bound to be painful in the church, and are always accompanied by a sense of failure; for after all, are we not supposed to be of one mind as well as one heart (1 Cor 1:10)? But in this world it does not always work out like that and some form of separation may be the only course in the short run. We ought to hold on to the hope that in the longer run the Lord will bring us to a place of agreement and reconciliation. But this process cannot be short-circuited.

Meanwhile the leader's resignation blew St Nicholas' music group apart. One of the group was soon going to have a baby and another was moving out of the village in any case. All at once we seemed to be back at square one, building up a worship group from scratch.

SEVEN

STAND

In the midst of all this Maureen and I finally went to Toronto. The Airport Vineyard Christian Fellowship had become world famous after the congregation had begun to experience extraordinary manifestations of the Holy Spirit. Since then both the church and the manifestations had been headline news in both the Christian and secular press. The publicity had generated controversy. People from all over the world had begun to go to Toronto simply in order to visit the Vineyard church; some to observe, others to worship.

'What's the purpose of your visit?' A bullet-headed, Canadian immigration officer was looking at Maureen and me as if we might be agents of the KGB. Certain people and certain questions seem to have the effect of putting you out of touch with yourself. This was one.

'To go to church,' I replied.

'How long are you staying.'

'Four days.'

'You've come all the way from England for four days just to go to church?' the officer said incredulously.

'Yes,' I answered, 'that's about it.'

This particular servant of the Dominion of Canada was

obviously unaware that more people were visiting Toronto to go to the Airport Vineyard than to go to Niagara Falls.

After a second interview with another immigration officer, Canada finally agreed to let us in, and we just had time to check in at our hotel before our first evening service at the Vineyard. The church had outgrown its original premises which were near the end of the airport runway, and had now acquired a new 'facility', only five minutes by taxi from the International Terminal. The building looked, both outside and in, like a vast supermarket, without the shelves. Instead of the shelves some 1500 chairs were set out, facing a central stage or platform with as much space again on all sides, covered in good thick carpet. The carpet, we were to discover, was an essential part of the furniture.

Every evening of the week there was a worship service, except Mondays. On Monday, it appeared, God was allowed to have a night off, or at least the resident team was. Every morning there was a seminar, covering some aspect of the current move of the Holy Spirit. Two or three afternoons a week there was a prayer meeting. With its own restaurant attached, serving cheap, simple but sustaining food, it was possible to do virtually everything at the Vineyard except sleep there. Maureen and I did just about that. For four days we practically lived at the church. We did not even make it to Niagara Falls.

It was not actually the sort of place you wanted to leave. There was a peace and an ease, a love and a joy which seemed to float in the air. Even at midnight, after the evening service, there would still be people sitting in the chairs, chatting in small groups, praying or being prayed for, worshipping or lying on the floor, apparently in no hurry to go home or back to their hotels.

Across the back of the auditorium hung a large banner carrying the church's mission statement: 'To walk in the love of God and to give it away'. This, the Airport Vineyard had now been doing on a huge scale for over a year. Each night 1500 – 2000 people gathered and at weekends up to 3000. After about forty-five minutes of singing there would be a roll-call. People were invited to stand as the name of their country or region on earth was called: Canada and USA of course; always a large contingent from England; others from Australia, New Zealand, Korea, Japan, Germany, Scandinavia; sometimes from Eastern Europe, India, Africa, China, South America. Christians from every denominations, Pentecostals, Baptists, Lutherans, Egyptian Copts, Catholics, and not a few of us Anglicans. Toronto is a Red Indian name meaning 'the meeting place'. The unity, so simple and unforced, of so many people from so many places coming to meet with God was profoundly moving.

After the roll-call came the testimonies: two or three people were invited to come up and tell what God had done for them over the previous few days. Time and again it was a story of a Christian leader, a pastor or priest, who had come to the Vineyard, burnt-out, discouraged, disillusioned, who had been re-envisioned and recharged, who had met with God in a new and life-changing way.

Each evening there was a sermon, not remarkable for either doctrine or delivery, but a simple exposition of some basic truth about God and about our relationship to him. The sermon would end with an invitation to anyone who did not know Jesus to come forward and receive that life and salvation which he offered. And always people would go forward, sixty, a hundred, two hundred.

Then, in a sense, came the moment we had all been waiting for: the ministry of the Holy Spirit. Anyone who wanted God to do something new or something more in their lives was invited to come out and line up on the carpet. The seats practically emptied. Maureen and I, like the rest, were out of our seats like sprinters out of the blocks. As the band sang and played, the ministry team moved slowly and quietly down the rows of waiting people.

Most people fell down, some fell backwards like trees going over, others just folded at the knees. Some started shaking, some shaking violently, others trembled or flapped their hands and arms, some were doubled over or developed strange jerks, a few might bounce up and down as if on springs, one or two thrashed about on the floor. Many laughed, some cried. Contrary to some of the rumours we had been told, nobody roared like a lion or barked like a dog. But this was the famous Toronto Blessing.

The first evening I gratefully collapsed into the arms of the catcher behind me as someone prayed for me. I was not at all sure whether this was the power of God or sheer fatigue after a day which had started for us over twenty hours earlier. It did not seem to matter. Here I was on the carpet in Toronto. 'You told me to come, and here I am,' I said to God. 'You know what you want to do while I am here. I am ready to receive it.'

The second evening I remained standing. I was not going to fall over just for the sake of it. A Canadian pastor was praying for me. 'What do you want God to do for you?' he asked.

'I don't really know,' I said, 'I want to know more of the love of God in my own life, and I want to be used more effectively by God in my ministry.' I then explained that I was an Anglican priest who had come over for just four days and I did not want to go home as I had come. I found myself explaining a bit about the trouble we were in at home because of what God was doing.

Wayne, who was praying for me, then moved behind me and told me he was removing arrows from my back, plucking them out, as it were, as he did so. I felt a palpable relief as he did this. I did not realise how much of a burden the situation at home had become for me, or how battered and bruised I felt.

Then Wayne began to pray the armour of God on to me, piece by piece. It sounded commonplace and hackneyed, but as he did so I actually felt each piece of armour on my body. The helmet was not hard and uncomfortable, but was lined with supple, old, leather and fitted my head like a glove. The breast-plate likewise was lined with leather. (Was such ancient armour lined with leather?) The sandals were well-worn to my feet and comfortable old friends. The shield was battered, but a proven defence. The sword was bright as I held it up; its thick handle filled my hand and it caught the sun with brilliant flashes of light. At that point God spoke to me the words of Ephesians 6:13, 'Therefore take the whole armour of God, that you may be able to withstand in the evil day, and having done all, to stand'. I did not fall down that night. I stood.

The third evening again we joined the prayer lines. This time I over-balanced backwards and was laid down on the carpet. I do not know how long I lay there, but for a long time I rested in the Spirit. I was aware of the band playing and the gentle songs that were being sung, 'Soften my heart, Lord', 'Unending love'. I worshipped in my spirit through the words and music. It was sufficient to be in his presence.

Our last night, Maureen and I had to leave the meeting before the time of ministry in order to catch our flight.

But we arranged to meet our new friend Wayne, the Canadian pastor, for more prayer beforehand. Both Maureen and I fell under the anointing of the Holy Spirit and side by side we both started to laugh, first a giggle, then laughter which had us rolling from side to side. It was nothing to do with humour, just a spring of joy that kept bubbling up from deep within.

Just another four days in the life of the Airport Vineyard, but for us one reminder after another that God was with us and knew our particular needs and loved us and wanted to bless us. He deals with everyone differently. For me, it was a gentle and reassuring experience, which restored and strengthened me to face the upheavals at home.

EIGHT

A RIVER TO SWIM IN

It was clear we had made some mistakes. It was a mistake to have introduced so many changes to the Sunday services at once. There had been a change of time, substantial changes in the order of service, a major change from having me presiding over all the services to a ministry shared much more equally between Stephen and myself. At St Nicholas', there was in addition the upheaval in the music group. All this, and the ministry of the Holy Spirit as well, had made people feel disorientated and insecure. Too many old landmarks had disappeared at once. It had all been too much. We should have introduced these changes more slowly, one step at a time. Perhaps, even more seriously, not enough explanation had been given to the congregations about these changes and the reasons for them, especially about the ministry of the Holy Spirit. I had to recognise and admit these mistakes and confess them both to God and to the congregations. We now had to back-track and put right some of the omissions.

I came to recognise that the ministry of the Holy Spirit is like swimming. Being surrounded by the Holy Spirit can feel like being surrounded by water for the first time.

It can be a strange and frightening environment to be in. I had assumed that by now our congregations were composed of swimmers. In fact that was not the case. Most had been near the water; some had paddled; but not all had learnt to swim in the river of God. Few people learn to swim by being pushed in at the deep end. Most non-swimmers have to go through a process of becoming accustomed to the water, learning the strokes, and practising in the shallow end first. The ministry of the Holy Spirit as an integral part of the main Sunday service would have to wait until we had prepared people better, and put in place some structures for supporting those who found the experience difficult or threatening. We had to have more swimming-lessons and get people used to the water first.

The Airport Vineyard in Toronto is not a parish church in rural England. If people visit the Airport Vineyard and are distressed or perturbed by what they see and hear, they do not go again. If they live in Toronto there are other churches for them to go to. If they live elsewhere, they return to the security of home. This is not to say that the staff at the Toronto Vineyard are not concerned about the effects of their ministry, only that they cannot and do not have to deal with all the repercussions. In our villages we had to live with all the consequences on our own doorstep. This meant, on the one hand, being able to share in all the excitement and joy of what God was doing; on the other hand, it meant having to help the people who were unhappy or offended.

Coming back from Toronto I decided to put the general ministry of the Holy Spirit on hold. If people wanted to come for such prayer and ministry personally they could be invited to come forward after the service, as they had done for several years. Meanwhile the more urgent task was to gather and calm the scattered flock.

When we arrived home the Body of Christ was in fact already at work healing itself. It was encouraging to find that people were spontaneously caring for one another. Leaders of house fellowships were gathering their own little flocks together: people were phoning up those they knew to be upset, calling round for a chat, lending each other helpful books. When a human body suffers some injury, the body at once goes into action to heal itself. Blood rushes to the scene of the injury carrying antibodies to fight infection, and proteins to repair the damaged parts. Likewise, if an ant-hill is disturbed, the colony at once mobilises itself to rebuild its nest. Ants converge on the site of the damage bringing materials and hands and feet to do the work of reconstruction. So it seemed the Body of Christ at home had spontaneously gone into action to treat and heal itself.

Peter and Margaret had moved into one of our villages, and started coming to church a year before. They had survived the culture shock of drums and guitars at St Nicholas', of people's arms and hands lifted up in worship, and had appreciated the warmth and friendliness of the congregation, the liveliness and enthusiasm of the people. Peter had been churchwarden in their previous village and both he and Margaret were used to village churches, but not quite like this.

They came to the next Alpha course, and sure enough on the 'Holy Spirit day' they met with God in a new and powerful way. They found it difficult to describe what had happened, but were awake most of the night talking about it to one another. This in itself was extraordinary, for although happily married for over twenty years they had never talked to each other before about God.

On a subsequent Alpha course Peter and Margaret had helped to lead a discussion group. On both Alpha courses they had witnessed other people being slain in the Spirit, and indeed Margaret herself had unexpectedly collapsed on the floor on one occasion overwhelmed by the power and peace of God. But yet, when these things began to happen on Sunday mornings Peter had found himself profoundly disturbed.

The leaders of their fellowship group were also called Peter and Margaret (a source of endless confusion to us all). This couple soon noticed that their namesakes were upset; they rang up and arranged to spend the afternoon together talking over what they all felt. Peter's past involvement with Freemasonry came to light. Peter was going to have to take time to reconsider the craft which at one time he had thought innocent and even benevolent. There was no instant resolution of Peter's unease at the manifestations of the Holy Spirit, but he and Margaret realised that their present difficulties were shared by others and that together we could work them through.

In time Peter renounced Freemasonry and the two couples held a ceremonial bonfire on which Peter's Masonic books and regalia were burnt. The relationships built up in the house fellowship proved strong enough to enable Peter and Margaret to survive this crisis. The personal trust between the two couples was enough to hold them within the fellowship of the church at a time when we were all having a rough ride.

As the principal pastor of these two churches, the primary responsibility for shepherding the flock was mine. I set to work on our return from Toronto visiting the hurt and disaffected. We planned some special meetings to teach people more fully about the ways of God in this present move of the Holy Spirit. But nothing I did could have replaced the loving care of the people for one another.

We did not recover everybody. Two or three couples who had been travelling in from towns and villages round about to worship with us, now decided that that was not such a good idea after all. One or two of our own parishioners also separated themselves from us. Others, like Peter and Margaret, decided to travel on with us.

I had always told people who were taking up some new work or ministry in our churches that they had my permission to make mistakes. After all, the person who never made a mistake never made anything. Making mistakes was part of learning. Now I had to avail myself of the same permission. I had made mistakes, and a leader's mistakes are usually highly conspicuous. But I did not suppose that any leader, any more than anyone else, did his job without making any mistakes. Only God never makes mistakes: we human beings often do. If we are to be used by God at all one of the things we have to overcome is the fear of making mistakes. God will forgive our mistakes, and if we are honest about them, most of our Christian brothers and sisters will too. God can even take our mistakes and redeem them, making them part of his plan for good. With God, making mistakes is not the end of everything.

NINE

IN DAYS LONG AGO

'I have been going to church for sixty or seventy years, and I have never seen that sort of thing going on before.'

I knew that Peggy had been offended. The first Sunday that we had stood and asked the Holy Spirit to come, I had suggested that those who wanted to do so should step out into the aisles so that the ministry team could pray with them. Several did, and soon it was difficult to step anywhere for the bodies on the ground. Peggy and her friend had wanted to leave and escape, but did not know how: if they stepped out into the aisle someone might pray for them!

Now, some weeks later, I was visiting Peggy at home and encouraging her to tell me what her feelings were:

'It does not seem right to me. I remember when I was a little girl I got told off for turning round in church, and now look at what they're doing. I thought church was supposed to be a place where you were reverent, not laughing and falling over and stamping your feet.'

I realised again what a lot we had been asking, especially of the older generation of worshippers. Ideas and habits inculcated by village school-masters, parsons, and parents were being contradicted and flouted. What right had I to come along and change the times and the ways for those who were worshipping in these country churches long before I was born?

The only justification could be Scripture. Did these things happen in the Bible? The things that we were seeing and hearing were certainly new to us, to me as well as to Peggy, but were they new to God? Had God had this sort of effect on people before?

There were the priests in the temple when it was dedicated by Solomon. 'The priests could not stand to minister because of the cloud; for the glory of the Lord filled the house of the Lord' (1 Kings 8:11 RSV). Whatever was going on there? Certainly more than we had been used to experiencing in any of our churches for sixty or seventy years. When had the vicar not been able to stand because of the manifest presence of the glory of God? And if the priests could not stand, what had they done, fallen down? Perhaps it had happened before, when the glory of the Lord came down upon the people. Does not Paul speak of the 'weight' of glory (2 Cor 4:17)? Perhaps people are sometimes weighed down by the glory of God and fall to the ground under that weight.

Then there was Daniel. The Lord himself appeared to Daniel by the river Tigris (Dan 10:2-11). The men who were with him did not see the vision but even they began to tremble violently at the presence of God. Daniel himself lost all his strength and fell down in a sort of trance as if he was fast asleep. Even when the Lord stood him up again he was still trembling.

Once we have seen these phenomena for ourselves, we find that all through the Bible people were falling down in the presence of God: Abraham (Gen 15:12), Ezekiel (Ezek 3:23), Peter, James and John (Matt 17:6), the soldiers in the garden of Gethsemane (Jn 18:6) and the soldiers at the tomb (Matt 28:4), Paul on the road to Damascus (Acts 9:4), and John on the island of Patmos (Rev 1:17). We may have thought at one time that such prostrations were entirely voluntary. Some of them certainly were not, and perhaps none of them were. Some of these characters fell forward on their faces, others fell backwards. Perhaps after all, falling over, one way or another, is quite a common effect of the manifest presence of God. If we are not used to people falling over in church, perhaps it is because we are not used to the presence of God in church.

The same can be said of laughing and crying. When God announced the birth of Isaac to Abraham his father, Abraham fell down and started laughing. It was not because he thought God had told a good joke. It was the release of a lot of pent up emotion. Abraham had waited and longed for a son and heir for so many years. Now he was to have one, and his relief and joy overflowed in laughter. Both laughter and tears can accompany the sudden release of emotion, sometimes both together. At the laying of the foundation stone of the second temple it was impossible to distinguish the sound of the shouts of joy from the sound of weeping (Ezra 3:11-13). These are natural reactions to moving experiences. If we are not used to people laughing and crying in church, perhaps it is because our religion has become so dry and cold that we are not being touched deeply by God at all.

There were other phenomena, which we had not yet seen or heard at St Nicholas' or St George's, but which people had heard about happening elsewhere. Staggering was something which Maureen and I had seen abundantly in Toronto. It could easily be mistaken for drunkenness. But that was precisely the impression the disciples had given on the day of Pentecost.

'These men are not drunk as you suppose,' Peter had to explain. 'It is only nine o'clock in the morning' (Acts 2:15). It could not have been the speaking in tongues that caused the crowd to suppose that the apostles were drunk. Jerusalem at such a time as Pentecost was an intensely polyglot city. People merely speaking foreign languages would not have caused any remark at all. When we go to Europe for our holidays we hear people speaking French or Italian. We do not suppose that they are drunk, merely that they must be French or Italian. The disciples were doing something other than speaking in tongues on the day of Pentecost, which caused people to suppose that they were drunk. If we are not used to seeing people staggering about in church as if they were drunk, perhaps it is because we are not used to people being filled with the Holy Spirit.

What is normal? Our own experience tends to be our standard of normality, and even of what is right and proper. But as Christians we constantly need to check our experience against the experience of God in Scripture. This will enable us to sort out the genuine from the weird or deviant. But it will also enable us to sort out where our own inherited norms have already deviated or fallen short of all that God has prepared for us. Our ideas of Christian normality need to be based on the life of the people of God in Bible times rather than on the life of the people of God in our own.

I talked this over with Peggy. 'Why didn't this happen years ago then, when we were young?' she said, 'Why is it only happening again now?'

To this question I did not and do not have an adequate answer, except in the sovereignty of God. I could point to the cycle of revival and decline in the history of God's people. I could point to the cycle in Scripture: how God would raise up leaders for his people Israel who would deliver them in times of trouble or bring them back into the ways of righteousness, but how, when the leader died, the people would revert to their bad old ways again (Judg 2:18-19). I could point to the same cycle in the story of the Christian church: how God has raised up prophets and preachers from age to age who have won thousands for the kingdom of God – Francis of Assissi or John Wesley – but how after a time the virtue of each revival has run out and the church has lapsed back into formalism and weakness.

It is the contention of those of us involved in the charismatic renewal that we are part of just such a new and sovereign moving of the Spirit of God in our own time. It is a bold claim to make; the credibility of the things that we are seeing today depends upon it being true, but the things that we are seeing give credibility to the claim.

TEN

—

HIS STRANGE WORK

In exile from the parish church, Peggy and her friend took refuge at the Methodist chapel in the village. They worshipped there on a Sunday morning, where people did not fall down or shake or laugh.

I could not help noticing the irony of this, and I suspect God had a wry smile about it too. For there was a time when the boot was on the other foot. The Methodist chapels came into existence in the first place because the 'excesses' of the Wesleyan revival were unacceptable in the parish churches. Now it appeared that the roles were reversed: people were going to the Methodists to escape from the 'excesses' of the Church of England!

The similarities between the happenings of the Wesleyan revival and the move of the Holy Spirit that we were experiencing were striking. At the beginning John Wesley himself was surprised at these manifestations of the power of God. It happened first some six months after his conversion. John Wesley, a number of his close companions and about sixty others were present at a 'love-feast' on 1st January 1739. Wesley records in his Journal:

About three in the morning, as we were continuing instant in prayer, the power of God came mightily upon us, insomuch that many cried out for exceeding joy, and many fell to the ground. As soon as we were recovered a little from that awe and amazement at the presence of His majesty we broke out with one voice, 'We praise Thee, O God; we acknowledge Thee to be the Lord.'

Then on 17th April soon after Wesley began his ministry in Bristol:

I went to Baldwin Street and expounded, as it came in course, the fourth chapter of the Acts. We then called upon God to confirm His word. Immediately one that stood by (to our no small surprise) cried out aloud, with the utmost vehemence, even as in the agonies of death. But we continued in prayer till 'a new song was put in her mouth, a thanksgiving unto our God.' Soon after, two other persons (well known in this place, as labouring to live in all good conscience towards all men) were seized with strong pain, and constrained to 'roar for the disquietness of their heart.' But it was not long before they likewise burst forth into praise to God their Saviour. The last who called upon God, as out of the belly of hell, was J(ohn) E(llis), a stranger in Bristol. And in a short space he also was overwhelmed with joy and love, knowing that God had healed his backslidings. So many living witnesses hath God given that His hand is still 'stretched out to heal,' and that 'signs and wonders are even now wrought by His holy child Jesus.' (Journal)

On 21st April

At Weavers' Hall a young man was suddenly seized with a violent trembling all over, and in a few minutes, the sorrows of his heart being enlarged, sunk down to the ground. But we ceased not calling upon God, till He raised him up full of 'peace and joy in the Holy Ghost.' (Journal)

Such phenomena soon became commonplace at Wesley's meetings both indoors and in the open air. As many then were offended at these manifestations of the power of God, as they are now.

We understood that many were offended at the cries of those on whom the power of God came; among whom was a physician, who was much afraid there might be fraud or imposture in the case. Today one whom he had known many years was the first (while I was preaching in Newgate) who broke out 'into strong cries and tears'. He could hardly believe his own eyes and ears. He went and stood close to her, and observed every symptom, till great drops of sweat ran down her face and all her bones shook. He then knew not what to think, being clearly convinced it was not fraud nor yet any natural disorder. But when both her soul and body were healed in a moment, he acknowledged the finger of God. (Journal 30th April)

Even the manifestation of laughter was experienced in those days. Once again it happened to Wesley himself first and then afterwards in one of his meetings.

I was a little surprised at some who were buffeted of Satan in an unusual manner by such a spirit of laughter as they could in no wise resist, though it was pain and grief unto them. I could scarce have believed the account they gave me had I not known the same thing ten or eleven years ago. Part of Sunday my brother and I then used to spend in walking in the meadows and singing psalms. But one day, just as we were beginning to sing, he burst out in a loud laughter. I asked him if he was distracted; and began to be very angry, and presently after to laugh as loud as he. Nor could we possibly refrain, though we were ready to tear ourselves in pieces, but we were forced to go home without singing another line. (Journal 9th May 1740)

In the evening such a spirit of laughter was among us that many were much offended. But the attention of all was fixed on poor L(ucretia) S(mith), whom we all knew to be no dissembler. One so violently and variously torn of the Evil One did I never see before. Sometimes she laughed till almost strangled; then broke out into cursing and blaspheming; then stamped and struggled with incredible strength, so that four or five could scarce hold her; then cried out, 'O eternity, eternity! Oh that I had no soul! Oh that I had never been born!' At last she faintly called on Christ to help her, and the violence of her pangs ceased.

Most of our brethren and sisters were now fully convinced that those who were under this strange temptation could not help it. Only E..th B.... and Ann H...n were of another mind, being still sure any one might help laughing if she would. This they declared to many on Thursday; but on Friday the 23rd God suffered Satan to teach them better. Both of them were suddenly seized in the same manner as the rest, and laughed whether they would or no, almost without ceasing. Thus they continued for two days, a spectacle to all; and were then, upon prayer made for them, delivered in a moment. (Journal 21st May 1740)

There are several different things going on here. One woman is clearly demonised, a situation which Wesley recognised and dealt with. But as to his own experience and that of the others, he is obviously perplexed. Wesley had learned from the Moravians a horror of 'levity'. Since laughter smacked to him of levity he was inclined to regard it as a temptation or a 'buffeting of Satan'. But he and Charles do not seem to have come to any harm by it, and John himself sounds more surprised than alarmed at the whole phenomenon.

Like those of us today who are held responsible for such happenings, Wesley was quizzed and cautioned about them constantly. He too had to consider his attitude to them:

> During this whole time I was almost continually asked, either by those who purposely came to Bristol to inquire concerning this strange work, or by my old or new correspondents, 'How can these things be?' And innumerable cautions were given me (generally grounded on gross misrepresentations of things), not to regard visions or dreams, or to fancy people had remission of sins because of their cries, or tears, or bare outward professions. To one who had many times written to me on this head, the sum of my answer was as follows:
>
> 'The question between us turns chiefly, if not wholly, on matter of fact. You deny that God does now work these effects; at least, that He works them in this manner. I affirm both; because I have heard these things with my own ears, and have seen them with my eyes. I have seen (as far as a thing of this kind can be seen) very many persons changed in a moment from the spirit of fear, horror, despair, to the spirit of love, joy, and peace; and from sinful desire, till then reigning over them, to a pure desire of doing the will of God. These are matters of fact whereof I have been, and almost daily am, an eye or ear witness. What I have to say touching visions or dreams, is this: I know several

persons in whom this great change was wrought in a dream, or during a strong representation to the eye of their mind, of Christ either on the cross, or in glory. This is the fact; let any judge of it as they please. And that such a change was then wrought appears (not from their shedding tears only, or falling into fits, or crying out: these are not the fruits, as you seem to suppose, whereby I judge, but) from the whole tenor of their life, till then many ways wicked; from that time holy, just, and good.' (Journal 20th May 1739)

Wesley was prepared to judge these strange manifestations of the Holy Spirit by their fruits. Were people's lives changed? If so, and they plainly were, then as far as Wesley was concerned, he would let God go on doing it his way, however bizarre his way might seem to the outside world or to the church.

ELEVEN

IT IS TRUE

Dear Martin,

I feel that I have to tell you that I am not enjoying the new Sunday services.

That is a pretty bland statement to make, but it sums up the plethora of other feelings which I am experiencing each week. Whereas I always used to leave church feeling uplifted and renewed, and ready to take on another week with God's help, now I have a tremendous desire to escape from the building, from the atmosphere, and from the people. *Not*, however, from God.

Having made my escape, I feel totally depressed, and I only start coming together again when I go back into church the next day and have a 'quiet word'.

My problem is particularly with the period of ministry of the Spirit. God doesn't keep coming to order like a computer program locked in a continuous loop. He doesn't, and would not want to frighten people away. Yet my daughter fled from the church in terror when someone fell down. Her's is a tentative faith, like a seedling pushing its way through dark earth in search of light and warmth. God would not want that seedling scorched by fear.

She is not alone. Others more mature are discomfited. They speak of hysteria and exhibitionism. Surely it must be right to nurture faith, not send it into clinical shock.

You lead a flock as an agent of Christ. I lead a flock of goats as a herdswoman. My goats trust me not to hurt them, they trust me not to make sharp noises around them which frighten them. If I introduce to the flock some action which induces fear they will scatter, and I will probably never regain their trust.

The goats cannot communicate by word or letter with me, but I can communicate to you the disquiet of a great many of your flock. I pray that you will find some way to explain.

Love, Hazel.

John and Hazel had been coming to church for a couple of years. John had appeared first, at the traditional service of Holy Communion at 8.00am. After a while he was at the more charismatic service at 9.30am as well, missing the awe but appreciating the joy. Then one night he retired to bed earlier than usual with my first book, *Speak to These Bones*. To his surprise he did not put it down until he had finished it, and then only after praying the prayer at the end in which he asked God to fill him with the Holy Spirit.

When he woke up the following morning he discovered that he had a new assurance in his faith. An intellectual understanding that Christ had died for all mankind had mysteriously turned into a personal conviction that Jesus had died for him. As time went by he found that old doubts which had long disturbed him had not been cleared up, but simply no longer seemed remotely relevant to his faith.

Meanwhile, Hazel was undergoing a pilgrimage of her own. Working away from home for much of the time, she was near the end of her tether. She had first met Jesus through an evangelical church in Glasgow in her youth. During a weekend away in the Trossachs she had had a powerful experience of God. But during the intervening thirty years so much had happened that had brought disillusionment and bitterness: two marriages, the first to a drunken husband, redundancy, and now a job which kept her 120 miles from home and lodging in a single room, had brought her to despair. She sat on her bed one Sunday morning and said, 'My father would not have let me go on like this.'

At once a television programme which had been interviewing Gorbachev changed to a simple church service from Holy Island. Feeling soothed and comforted, Hazel picked up the local paper and saw an advertisement for a cottage to rent. She phoned at once and got it, a little haven of peace. Her heavenly Father had heard her cry. Hazel knew that this was the God she had met with so long ago in the Trossachs coming to fetch her home again now.

So, soon Hazel was coming to church with John. The onset of ME meant that she had to leave her job completely, and God began to show them the future he had planned for them together: poorer financially but richer spiritually. They became accustomed to St George's and began to appreciate the fellowship of the congregation and the liveliness of the worship. Then the services changed and I received Hazel's agonised letter.

I went to see them. Clearly the issue of newcomers, visitors, and those still young in the faith had to be taken seriously. If we were to integrate the ministry of the Spirit into the Sunday morning service again we would have to put in place some structure for looking after the 'non-swimmers'. Equally clearly there were other issues which were troubling John and Hazel themselves. I dealt with these as best I could on my visit, but left feeling somewhat discouraged. Much seemed to be left unresolved.

This however was one which God undertook to deal with by himself. John told the tale in a subsequent edition of the church newsletter.

My daughter had fled from St George's terrified at what her husband had described as something utterly bizarre. I had been asked by neighbours why the ministry team never seemed to 'do carpet time'. I could not understand why it was always the same people who collapsed at the thought of a prayer, and generally the appearance of artificiality and contrivance totally put me off. Nevertheless when Hazel, my wife, read in the local newspaper that some people from the Airport Vineyard in Toronto were addressing a meeting in St Andrew's Hall on the following Tuesday, I decided, with some reluctance, to accompany her and hear what they had to say – straight from the horse's mouth. (This was despite the presence of a very painful back brought on by a surfeit of gardening and made worse by a surfeit of churchyard clearance.)

There were a lot of people there, most of whom looked perfectly normal – but there, you never can tell from appearances can you?

In we went and there was a time of worship. There is a time and a place for dancing an Irish jig, I thought, and it isn't when we are singing hymns. Still the rendition of *Holy, Holy, Holy, Lord God Almighty* starting as it did very quietly and very slowly, then quickening and developing into a wonderful crescendo of sound, left the heart pulsating with praise.

Steve Long then spoke – with a clarity which was a joy to hear.

'If you look at what is happening,' he said, 'it looks completely bizarre' (where had I heard that word used before?) 'but if God reveals the depth of his love for you, what could be more natural than that you should weep? If he lays his joy on your heart, what could be me natural than that you should laugh? If he pours his peace upon you, what could be more natural than that you lie down?' The point got through to my head.

Steve concluded his address with some words on healing and then proposed that a healing session be held, first for people experiencing back pain. Now I don't want to appear rude about the quality of seating in St Andrew's Hall but I promise you that after an hour on one of their hard chairs, my back was screaming.

'Go on,' said Hazel, 'or else shut up about your bloomin' back.'

'We'll deal with the men first,' said Steve from the platform.

With the biblical picture in my head of man followed by camel followed by wife, I was persuaded to go through to the cloisters where the backs were to be done.

I was third in the queue. The first man received ministry and stayed on his feet (I can cope with this I thought), then came number two. He was a big man, he moaned, groaned and crashed to the floor.

'I really do not want to be here,' I thought, but having reached the front of the queue, it seemed awfully rude to turn round and walk off. I stayed – well, you would, wouldn't you?

Then it was my turn.

It wasn't the first time I had been prayed for in this manner and in the way that had happened before I felt myself swaying. (Stand there with your eyes closed and your hands out in an unnatural position and what else do you expect?) I fought, God knows I fought, but it somehow seemed to grow terribly dark and I felt as if something about a foot round was pushing me in the middle of my chest.

'OK Lord – your will not mine.'

I was flat on my back with an almost peach coloured luminosity growing and growing in intensity until it reached a brilliance in which I knew I was in the presence of my Lord.

A hand held me to the floor, pressing gently. I opened my eyes – no one near me. I closed my eyes – still brilliance, still a massive outpouring of love.

Slowly, but all too soon, it faded. I got up, I went home, I rejoiced. I rejoiced that even the most suspicious can be shown a new way, even the most cynical can be brought to heel. The point got through to my heart.

Conclusions and summaries are not easy but it seems to me that each of us has our own small road to Damascus to travel, and that each receives their own small miracles along the way.

In terms of God one thing is however crystal clear, if I may pinch a word from Marx of all people, 'You have nothing to fear but fear itself, nothing to lose but your chains.'

PS My back got healed too.

John

At 10.30pm that Tuesday evening, the Tuesday after Easter, the lights were still burning in St Nicholas' church. We had been holding the first of our two meetings to explain to the parishioners the things we had experienced in Toronto and to pass on to them some of the teaching that we had received there. The chancel-room floor was still covered in bodies. At one time the bodies had been wall to wall, but some people had gone home and now only a few remained. John and Hazel came panting up the path and burst in, full of what had just happened to them at St Andrew's Hall.

On the first Easter evening two of Jesus' disciples had walked out to Emmaus and on the way had had a wonderful encounter with the risen Lord. Hastening back to Jerusalem straightaway they had found the rest of the disciples gathered together in the upper room. 'It is true,' they had said, 'the Lord has risen' (Lk 24:33-35). It seemed just like that to us.

—

TWELVE

HOW MUCH MORE...

'I must admit I was frightened. Or I was at first. It seemed to be out of control. I did not know who was in control. If anyone was.'

Wendy had come to the meeting at St Nicholas' on the same Tuesday evening. She and her husband Roger had listened to what had been said and had stayed during the ministry of the Holy Spirit. Afterwards Wendy said, 'I am not actually frightened any more, but I still don't see the point. What would God want to do that for? Why should he make people fall down or laugh or cry like that?'

Fear at the manifestations of the Holy Spirit is not uncommon and is legitimate. We needed to address it. In fact it is not one fear but several, in different mixtures in different people. But they are all related to the question of control. It is indeed a dangerous thing to overthrow the mechanisms of control either social or personal. From childhood onwards human beings have a deep need to know that someone is in control.

There is the need for self-control. Not only is this inculcated and taught to us from an early age, but it is actually a fruit of the Spirit (Gal 5:23). So what is happening when, in the name of the Holy Spirit himself, people seem to be losing their self-control? We are afraid, and rightly so, of many of the lusts and passions that lurk within us. We have had to learn to control our anger, our jealousy, our greed, our sexuality. Some people have more of a problem with these passions than others. Some people can afford to be relatively relaxed about them; others are sitting, as it were, on top of a volcano which constantly threatens to erupt under them, causing goodness-knows-what havoc to themselves and other people. Some people are instinctively afraid of what might happen if their personal lid ever came off: 'What will happen if I let go?'

Such apprehension takes on another dimension again when we are in the company of other people. However stable I may think I am personally, I am aware of the instability of others. Mass emotion can indeed be a powerful and terrifying force. People becoming highly emotional around us or losing their own self-control causes most of us to feel uncomfortable and unsafe. This is both a psychological and a spiritual phenomenon. There are indeed supernatural forces at work, and there are spirits which are far from benign which can all too easily take control both of individuals and of groups. If people start to behave in strange ways and to surrender their self-control to outside spiritual forces, we do well to question what these outside forces are.

Even in a rural church, people were in touch with the wider Christian scene. They read the papers and Christian magazines; some belonged to other Christian organisations. Wendy, and others in the parishes, were aware that controversy surrounded these spiritual manifestations. Some Christian leaders had spoken out against them. Were these manifestations of God or were they the work of the devil? Were they true manifestations of the power of the Holy Spirit, or were they part of some Satanic delusion?

In any case, why would God want to do such things? The Bible says that 'everything should be done in a fitting and orderly way' (1 Cor 14:40). Particularly in the Church of England we had been used to worship which was solemn and dignified. These manifestations of the Holy Spirit were neither orderly, solemn nor dignified. Could that be God?

That of course was the ultimate question: was this God? But God had given us the means to answer this question. Faced with the problem of discerning spirits in his own generation, Isaiah wrote:

> When men tell you to consult mediums and spiritists, who whisper and mutter, should not a people enquire of their God? Why consult the dead on behalf of the living? To the law and to the testimony! If they do not speak according to this word, they have no light of dawn (Is 8:19-20).

Once again we came back to the need to test the phenomena in the light of Scripture. When we find that people in the Bible do testify to these manifestations in their encounters with God we can say at least that this *may* be God. But it is important to see how far this argument can take us. Someone laughing on the ground may be manifesting a work of God (Gen 17:17), but equally she may not (Lucretia Smith). Even in one meeting one person may be under the power of the Holy Spirit, and another under the power of another spirit. We shall need other means of discernment than a simple appeal to Scripture to sort out which is which. But Scripture shows us that it *may* be God.

Jesus was addressing this very issue of fear of the Holy Spirit when he said:

> Which of you fathers, if your son asks for a fish, will give him a snake instead? Or if he asks for an egg, will give him a scorpion? If you then, though you are evil, know how to give good gifts to your children, how much more will your Father in heaven give the Holy Spirit to those who ask him! (Lk 11:11-13).

This is the faith on which this ministry of the Holy Spirit must be based: that when we ask God to give us the Holy Spirit we receive the Holy Spirit and not some other spirit, and that whatever we receive from the Holy Spirit is good and not bad. In this passage Jesus clearly teaches us to ask for the Holy Spirit, and even to ask repeatedly as children ask repeatedly for food. We are also to ask with the childlike faith that our heavenly Father will see to it that we get an egg and not a scorpion, a fish and not a poisonous snake. The faith that we need to maintain in this ministry of the Spirit, sometimes against all appearances, is that God is in charge and that God knows what he is doing.

This ministry does involve a certain loss of control. Individually, we surrender our self-control to God; we let the Holy Spirit come and take control. This is in fact what is meant by self-control as a fruit of the Spirit. It is not our ordinary, old, human, self-control, but a new sort of self-control that comes from being controlled by the Holy Spirit. That may be different from our own ideas of self-control. This is the only situation in which it can be right to surrender our self-control: when we are surrendering it to God.

We are right to be wary of our inner drives and emotions. We are right to be wary of what will happen to us and to other people if we simply let it all hang out. But we need not be fearful of what will happen when we surrender our self-control to God. He can cope with our emotions even if we cannot. He can control us even if we cannot control ourselves. He will hold us together even though we feel we are falling apart. Or at least, he will put us back together after we have fallen apart.

What is happening in these times of Holy Spirit ministry is very often precisely that. God is releasing in us pent up emotions of anger, grief, hurt and fear which we have simply not been able to cope with ourselves. It can look distressing; it can sound alarming; it can be upsetting at the time for those looking on. But if God is doing it, it is good, indeed it is profoundly healing; it is bringing a new liberty and a new wholeness to that person. The answer to the question of why God should do such a thing is quite simply that that is precisely what that person needs.

It is also a surrender of self-control which remains strictly voluntary. We allow the Holy Spirit to come and take control, voluntarily. God does not at any point override my will; he accepts it and respects it. Even if I have invited the Holy Spirit to come upon me, and even if I have begun, for example, to jerk or shake, I can stop the manifestation of the Spirit if I want to. The ministry of the Holy Spirit involves a continuous cooperation between him and me. We are not ultimately out of control.

What applies to the individual applies also to the service or meeting as a whole. When the Holy Spirit is invited to come, the minister or leader surrenders direct control over what happens next. That in itself requires a level of faith in the minister. Many clergy and church leaders feel threatened by charismatic renewal because it involves losing control of what is happening in the church. This comes into particularly sharp focus in the ministry-of-the-Spirit time. For the minister it is an exercise in giving God back his church, and allowing him to be God and to take control. But it can be scary.

There are temptations in both directions for the leader, as for others. There is the temptation to give God a hand, to manipulate proceedings, to add a bit of extra hype. But not only are most people extremely wary of such manipulation but any manifestations produced in such a way are simply false and counter-productive. With this ministry God does not need any help.

There is the contrary temptation to close the whole thing down as soon as anybody in the meeting becomes a bit noisy or boisterous: announce another hymn or tell them to be quiet. It is possible that some of the manifestations are the result of over-enthusiasm or exhibitionism on the part of some in the congregation. But the wheat and the tares are so alike that to try to weed out the tares will result in pulling up the wheat as well. For the most part things have to be left to go on as they are, side by side, some manifestations of God and some perhaps of the flesh.

It is also possible that some manifestations are manifestations of unclean spirits. When Jesus came into a place the power of his very presence sometimes caused the demons to cry out. So when the Holy Spirit comes into a place, his very presence sometimes causes the demons to cry out. But the demons were already there in the first place. They came in with demonised people. They have not arrived to take possession of people when the Holy Spirit was invited. The manifestation of those unclean spirits is not actually evil in itself. Whatever the Holy Spirit causes to happen is good. The evil spirits are caused to manifest themselves so that they may be driven out.

As with the individual, the minister or leader of the meeting remains and needs to be seen in ultimate control. As God continues to respect the will of the individual, so God, in an amazing way, respects the will of the appointed leaders of his church. If a leader says that he does not want manifestations of the Spirit in his church, then the Holy Spirit will take the hint and stay away. If the leader asks the Holy Spirit to stop, then the Holy Spirit will stop.

During the ministry of the Holy Spirit the leader needs to remain available to deal with what happens. Unclean spirits may need to be identified and dealt with appropriately. A disruptive person may need to be restrained or taken aside. The sheep need to know that their shepherd watches over them. This matter of control needs to be addressed and people need reassurance. God is in control and God knows what he is doing. Under him a trusted and trustworthy minister is in control. It is safe to let go and let God be God.

THIRTEEN

A TREE IS RECOGNISED
BY ITS FRUIT

Jesus said, 'Make a tree good and its fruit will be good, or make a tree bad and its fruit will be bad, for a tree is recognised by its fruit' (Matt 12:33).

They say in Toronto that it is not how they go down that counts, but how they get up. Wesley said, 'not from their shedding tears only, or falling into fits, or crying out, these are not the fruits whereby I judge, but from the whole tenor of their life.' The final test of this ministry does not lie in the outward and visible manifestations, be they sensational or not, but in the results in a person's character and daily life.

This, we shall often never know unless we take the opportunity and the trouble to find out. It is no impertinence to enquire afterwards, 'what was going on while you were on the floor? What was God doing?'

Dianne was one of those whose laughter had caused some offence in church. She had indeed, on more than one occasion, been helpless with laughter, rolling on the ground and mopping her eyes. What was God doing then? It was some months before I heard the whole story.

Over thirty years before, at the age of eight, Dianne's

mother had tried to commit suicide. Dianne had not been allowed to know more than the bare and shocking fact, though she had a clear memory of her older brother throwing away in anger the bottle of pills which her mother had taken. The fear and horror, the confusion and guilt had been things which eight-year-old Dianne had been unable to cope with. She had shut the door on the memory, as one might shut the door with a shudder on a cupboard in which one had found a particularly large and hairy spider. But of course that means that the door is almost impossible to open ever again.

A second trauma had followed, and then a third. At the age of twenty-five Dianne had miscarried and lost a baby at four and a half months. With two older children to look after she had had to carry on as if nothing had happened. She was never able to grieve properly for the child she had never borne. But she had felt a desperate sense of loss in her heart, a loss which had not been properly acknowledged or expressed. That too was still locked away inside her: the cork had been put in the bottle and the bottle put away to collect dust.

Then eight years later again, a brother-in-law had been suddenly killed in a car crash. The police had come first to Dianne and asked her to take the responsibility of breaking the awful news both to the widow and to the parents. As before, Dianne had had to be the one who carried on and helped other people to cope while her own feelings were suppressed. Her own shock and grief had never been acknowledged. She herself had never had time to face and resolve her own inner turmoil – until it was too late. When everyone else's grief was over, there was another closed door in Dianne's life, closed on unfinished business.

The Holy Spirit took Dianne to each of these doors in

turn. He opened them for her and he kept control while all the tensions and shocks came pouring out. All the observer saw or heard was laughter and tears, both God-given mechanisms of release. Counselling over a long period of time might have been able to achieve the same effect, had Dianne ever sought such help. But the divine Counsellor did in as many minutes what a human counsellor might have achieved in hours, if at all.

It was not very dignified for Dianne. But then God does not seem to care as much about our dignity as we do. What God cares about is our happiness and our wholeness, and he has his own supremely effective methods of ministering these things to us. Certainly Dianne was not complaining about her treatment. God had given her blessings of which she had not really known her own need. He had known her needs better than she had. But she finally stood up feeling a new woman, light and free; free of loads she had hardly realised she was carrying and with a new lightness of heart and spirit.

Georgina was over eighty, a frail-looking, white-haired old lady. She had suffered with deafness for some years and was delighted when St Nicholas' church installed an induction loop. Her hearing-aid could now pick up the preacher's voice with perfect clarity. Georgina was one of the first to be filled with the Holy Spirit at St Nicholas', which always proved to us that openness to God was not a matter of age. She came regularly to church and to the Saturday evening celebrations that we held once a month.

On one of these Saturday evenings I invited everyone as usual to stand and be open to receive the Holy Spirit. For some it might be for the first time, for others it would simply be a matter of going on being filled with the Spirit. Jesus, as we read about him in the gospels, comes and goes (Jn 16:28). The Holy Spirit, as we read about him in the New Testament, comes and comes. So he came again that night.

As Georgina stood with open hands and closed eyes she heard a clear command, 'Take that hearing-aid out of your ear.' No one was praying for her specifically; the church was otherwise quiet. Immediately she did as she was told, took the aid out of her ear and sat down hard on the pew feeling very weak. A moment or two later I started speaking to the congregation again, and Georgina realised that she was hearing every word I said with her own unaided ears. The joy of recovering the natural hearing that she thought she had lost for ever continued to light up Georgina's face for weeks afterwards.

Strangely, five months later, she contracted a severe infection in her body which made her ill for several weeks. During this time her deafness returned. I do not pretend to know what exactly is going on in such incidents. That God touched Georgina's ear and sovereignly restored her hearing that night, I am in no doubt. That he could do so again, I am in no doubt. Why her deafness returned, I do not know.

Georgina also came to the meeting on the Easter Tuesday evening after our return from Toronto. She was one of those slain in the Spirit, although, being in her eighties, she was not naturally inclined to falling over. As she fell, she felt on the contrary that she was being lifted up. Up and up, and as she floated up the heavens seemed to open and she saw myriads of angels. 'Ye holy angels bright'; these were indeed very bright. Then the throng of angels parted and she saw the figure of Jesus. Her heart was filled with inexpressible joy.

After a while the vision faded and Georgina sat up. She found Maureen and Christine sitting beside her and blessing what God was doing. 'I've been to heaven,' she said, 'I really have'. Then she lay down again and the vision was repeated to her just as before.

The whole experience left an impression on Georgina of the nearness of Jesus. It continued afterwards to have the power to fill her with joy. She had always lived a godly life and her years had been happy ones, but as the days went by now she found her walk with the Lord becoming closer and closer; as she could do less and less for herself she found the Lord doing more and more for her.

These are the sort of things God does. He does heal the broken-hearted and set the prisoners free (Is 61:1). He does make the deaf hear (Mk 7:37). He does catch people up into heaven to see and hear things which cannot be uttered (2 Cor 12:2-4). As I look at these things I can confidently say, 'This is God'. If there were some strange things going on while God was doing it, if people were laughing or crying or falling over, does that matter? Who am I to tell God how to do his business? If that is the way he wants to do it, that is the way he wants to do it. I am his servant. I simply rejoice at what he does.

FOURTEEN

GO INTO YOUR ROOM

The longer term effects of Toronto on my own life were also surprising. The senior pastor at the Vineyard, John Arnott, in telling the story of how God had dealt with him, had recalled that one day God had said to him, 'John, give me your mornings.'

Most Christians will be familiar with the way in which God can take a few simple words, sometimes from Scripture, sometimes like these from a sermon, sometimes from a casual conversation with a friend, and use them to open up whole new horizons of understanding and change our lives for ever. Such words were these. I suddenly understood that God wanted some of my time each day to himself. I had never seen my prayers in that light before.

At theological college, I had been taught and trained to pray. I had learned various techniques of biblical meditation. I had always faithfully recited the daily services of the Church of England, Morning and Evening Prayer. I had always done these things as a duty, believing that whether I might feel like it or not, these exercises were doing me good. Indeed there were many times when I knew they were: I was aware of the blessing of God.

There were many times when my prayers were sweet to me.

There were of course other times when my prayers were dry and arid, when it was difficult or impossible to stop myself from day-dreaming or my thoughts from wandering. But I never gave up. Apart from the formal daily services, I reckoned to pray for half an hour each day. But especially of late the pressure of other engagements and of parish administration had been crowding in on my prayer-time, and sometimes days would go by together without my finding any time for God himself. I knew that this should not be, and I knew that I was the poorer for it, but neither of these motives was strong enough to make any difference.

Then John Arnott's words hit me. Not that God was saying to me that he wanted my mornings exactly, but I understood that God wanted to spend time with me each day. That turned my understanding, not just of my prayers, but of my whole life, on its head. Up till then I had supposed that it was for my own benefit that I prayed. All of a sudden I saw that I spent time with God to please him.

In a way which I still find astonishing I came to see the whole history of the world, the story of the human race, and the work of redemption in a new light. It was there in the Bible staring me in the face but I had never seen it like this before.

Right at the beginning God had created human beings because he wanted their love and friendship. It was not that he was lonely, because the Holy Trinity is from eternity to eternity a fellowship of love. But just as the love of husband and wife overflows in the procreation of children, to enlarge the fellowship of their love, so God had created human beings to enlarge the fellowship of his love.

Then our first ancestors had spurned him. They had rebelled against him, decided to go their own way, cutting themselves off from fellowship with him. I suddenly understood the infinite pathos of those words God had spoken in the garden of Eden, 'Where are you?' (Gen 3:9). I suppose it depends on the tone of voice with which you hear them said. Up to now, I guess, I had imagined God speaking in the tone of an angry headmaster, 'Where are you, boy?' Now I understood that it was the tone of lost love. God it seemed had been used to meeting the man and the woman in the garden in the cool of the day, and enjoying their company after their work was done. It was their 'prayer-time'. Then one evening God came to keep his nightly appointment with his friends, and they were not there. I believe God's heart was breaking as he called out, 'Where are you?'

But knowing, of course, all that had happened from the beginning and all that was to happen, God that day put into operation a plan of redemption; a plan to win back for himself the sons of Adam. Throughout history God has been looking for people to be his friends. In Abraham, God found a man who was again willing to obey him and trust him, and so Abraham was called the friend of God (Jas 2:23). In Moses God found a man with whom he could converse as frequently and as easily as a man speaks to his friend (Ex 33:11). At the climax of his ministry Jesus could say to his disciples 'You are my friends' (Jn 15:14-15).

For the first time I understood that the whole point of God saving me, of Jesus dying for me, was so that I could be a friend of God. It was not, first of all, that I wanted to be his friend (actually I did not at first), but that he wanted to be my friend. I loved him because he first loved me. I knew the Scripture (1 Jn 4:19), but somehow I had never understood the full implication of it.

For the first time also I understood the Scripture which says, 'I, the Lord your God, am a jealous God' (Ex 20:5). Of course he is: just as a friend or even a lover is jealous, he is jealous. Scripture goes even further than likening our relationship to God to that of friends: it likens it to that of lovers, the bridegroom and the bride. 'Let him kiss me with the kisses of his mouth…My lover is mine and I am his' (Song 1:1 and 2:16). Daring stuff, and difficult to handle, especially perhaps for males. But there it is, as a figure of speech, and it applies to our relationship to God. Just as I had been jealous if I had seen my girlfriend flirting with another man, or worse still if she had been going out with another man, so was God jealous of me. In the Old Testament he was always jealous of his people giving their love and their worship to idols. He is still jealous if our hearts are fixed on anything else but him.

So he wanted some of my time for himself: that was the point of my prayer-time. It did not seem to me that he was asking me to give him my whole mornings, as he had asked John Arnott, but it did seem to me that he was asking me for two hours each day. This seemed to be impossible to me. How was I to find an extra two hours in the day for prayer? I knew that all the real saints had got up early in the morning and spent hours alone with God before the day began, but I had tried that. At various times in my life I had tried to get up earlier to pray and it had always been a dismal failure. I could sustain it for a week or two but then I would be so tired that I could not go on. The two hours had to be fitted in to my normal waking day if they were to be fitted in at all.

The key, I discovered, was to ignore the phone and the door. It was not too difficult to find two hours sometime during the day to disappear upstairs. There, I started to do as Jesus had said: 'When you pray, go into your room, close the door and pray to your Father, who is unseen' (Matt 6:6). Believing that God himself was jealous of this time I spent with him, I ignored the ringing of the phone or the door-bell. If Maureen was at home, well and good: she could tell callers that I was not available. If everyone else was out, too bad: people could call again. This went against a good deal of what both the world and the church had taught me; was I not supposed to be available, especially to anyone who might be in need? But I had learned a new priority, to be available to the lover of my soul.

These two hours have become an oasis in the business of every day, till I wonder how I have survived without them for so long. In some mysterious way the same amount of work still seems to get done in the hours that remain. God's economy with time, as well as with money, seem to work in a different way from the world's. Many times I have been tempted to shorten the time; perhaps only one and a half hours today. But I have learned that God knows best, and that for me at least two hours is the right time. It is often in the last half an hour in which God gives me most of himself.

There are still times when the presence of God is sweet and immediate, and other times when for me at least there is less obvious reward. But then I am not there for my own pleasure but for his. I try to give him my attention. I read a chapter of the Bible and ask him to speak to me through it. That never fails, and I always go away refreshed by some insight into his ways. I can talk over with him the problems and the people on my mind. I can relax and unwind, and hear what he has to say to me. And I am constantly awed that he should feel like that about me, that this time together is so precious to him.

FIFTEEN

ONE FLESH

All this time ordinary daily life went on: the post was delivered; the cows were milked; the mothers took the children to school, and collected them each afternoon; babies were born; old people died and were buried; couples were married.

Some of those marriages ran into difficulties. The statistics were probably much the same as in other parts of the country. Divorce is one of the plagues of our times, in villages as much as in towns. Every so often there would be fresh gossip about who was having an affair with whoever-else's wife. It was hardly a scandal, just another family breaking up.

In the years that I had been the rector of St Nicholas' and St George's we had been surrounded by this rising tide of matrimonial breakdown, but it had not, until recently, started to lap over the dyke into the churches. But all of a sudden we seemed to have a veritable flood of marriage problems within our two congregations. I could soon count eight couples whose marriages were in serious trouble.

Anyone who has ever tried to help people in this situation will know how intractable the problems seem to be:

the mutual recriminations, the differences of perception, the hidden agendas. There is no reason to suppose that these problems are any different from those which previous generations faced, but people's reaction to them certainly is. Today, the secular culture encourages and expects couples simply to walk away from their difficulties. The world knows only two alternatives: stay and be miserable for the rest of your life, or leave and hope for a better time with somebody else. The third alternative, staying and changing, both yourselves and your relationship, does not even appear above the horizon.

One of the principle services the church can perform for a godless society is to provide examples of alternatives, to establish a counter-culture, to be a place where people do things differently. In the context of marriage, we need to provide models of how to work through matrimonial problems together, of how to forgive, of how to find healing for our mutual hurts. There are ways of handling these situations which do not merely reproduce the cycle of brokenness and insecurity in yet another generation. But all of a sudden we were not doing very well at it: many of our own couples, mostly new Christians, but not in the first flush of enthusiasm, were now struggling to hold their marriages and families together.

One of the most baffling factors was that it was often the women who were breaking up the family. Traditionally it was the man who would tire of the little woman at home, and take off after someone more exciting or flattering to himself. But in a majority of cases it now seemed to be the wives who would not put up with husbands who were less than perfect. Until recently women were locked into marriage by financial dependency. But automatic welfare benefits and housing allowances for single parents have changed all that, not to mention women with careers and incomes of their own. Now the feminist pendulum seemed to have swung to the opposite extreme: here were women married to husbands who genuinely wanted to make their marriages work, husbands who were willing to change and adapt, but whom their wives seemed determined to junk. The women were filing for divorce.

When Jesus was asked about divorce he said, 'What did Moses command you?' What Moses had commanded the people of Israel was what God had commanded him; the law of Moses was, under that dispensation, the law of God. The Pharisees told Jesus, 'Moses permitted a man to write a certificate of divorce and send his wife away.' Jesus answered,

> It was because your hearts were hard that Moses wrote you this law. But at the beginning of creation God made them male and female. For this reason a man will leave his father and mother and be united to his wife, and the two will become one flesh. So they are no longer two but one. Therefore what God has joined together, let man not separate (Mk 10:29).

Jesus confirmed the teaching of Genesis 2:18-24: sex, or gender, is God's creation, and his purpose is fulfilled in the life-long union of a man and a woman: that is, marriage.

From the beginning God's plan was for a life-long union of a man and a woman. God hates divorce (Mal 2:16). But because of human sin, because of the hardness of human hearts, God allowed for divorce in the law of Moses. That is to say, that God recognised that in the sinful state divorce may be the lesser of two evils; it may be better for everyone concerned that husband and wife should separate, rather than continue fighting and hurting each other and their children in a loveless marriage. Thus the law of Moses permitted divorce, and for the same reasons, the law of the land permits divorce today.

But for Christians there is a third alternative. God promised,

> I will sprinkle clean water on you, and you will be clean; I will cleanse you from all your impurities and all your idols. I will give you a new heart and put a new spirit within you; I will remove from you your heart of stone, and give you a heart of flesh. And I will put my Spirit in you and move you to follow my decrees and be careful to keep my laws (Ezek 36:25-27).

This prophecy is fulfilled when we believe in Jesus, are born again of water and the Spirit, and made a new creation.

How, then, can Christians seek divorce? Their hearts are not hard any more, so that they have to separate from one another. The Holy Spirit in them moves them to fulfil God's original purpose, to be faithful to one another until death parts them. A Christian unequally yoked to an unbeliever may still find it necessary to invoke the permission to divorce (1 Cor 7:15), but a Christian couple have no need of such a way out. God can work out in them his perfect plan.

Richard and Ruby had been married for over twenty years. But in the last two years their marriage had been going through a bad time. Richard was subject to chronic anxiety and bouts of depression. He was worn out with worries about money, about keeping his job, about paying the mortgage. When minor incidents annoyed him at home, he was already at the end of his tether and lost his temper easily. Ruby was the one who bore the brunt of

Richard's increasing rages. Richard threw crockery, broke furniture, and spent days in sullen, speechless anger. Eventually Ruby made plans to leave him: she secretly packed boxes and arranged a bolt-hole. Another row blew up, and Ruby finally announced that she was going.

Richard walked out to find time to think. He went down to the farm where they bought their milk. Margaret saw him coming. 'Hello, Richard,' she called out. 'Are you all right?'

'Yes,' Richard replied. 'Well, no actually. Ruby's leaving me.'

'Come on in,' Margaret said. 'Tell me all about it.'

So Richard told her the story of their marriage and his increasing anger and depression. 'Let's pray about it, shall we?' Margaret said, 'I'll fetch Peter too.' So Peter came in from feeding the cows and together they prayed for Richard and Ruby's marriage.

A few days later Margaret called on Ruby and heard her side of the story. She prayed with her too, while the tears streamed down Ruby's face. 'Why don't you both come to church on Sunday?' Margaret said.

Neither Richard nor Ruby had been to church for many years, Richard not since he had been a choir boy and altar-server in his youth. 'OK I'll come with you if you want,' Richard said, 'though I don't suppose it will do us any good.' But it did. That very first Sunday God worked a miracle; Richard and Ruby came out of church different people.

'Shall we give it another go then?' Richard had said. 'Yes, if you want to,' Ruby had replied.

Richard and Ruby went on coming to church. They joined house fellowships. They came to the Alpha course. They were filled with the Holy Spirit, and their marriage never looked back. God spoke powerfully to Richard through some words of Jesus in John 6: 'I am the bread of life. He who comes to me will never go hungry, and he who believes in me will never be thirsty... All that the Father gives me will come to me, and whoever comes to me I will never drive away' (vv 35,37). Richard realised that God was giving him a new start. He found the realisation overwhelming. With it came a peace which passed all understanding. His anxieties disappeared; his depressions disappeared; his tempers disappeared. God gave Richard a new heart; he also gave Ruby a new heart. God restored their marriage; more than that, God gave them a better marriage than they had ever had before. God can do it.

—

SIXTEEN

DRIVE OUT DEMONS

There were three principle activities in the ministry of Jesus: he preached the gospel, healed the sick and cast out demons (Matt 4:23-24). When he sent out the Twelve he gave them the same instructions. 'Preach the gospel, heal the sick and drive out demons' (Matt 10:7-8). There has been a recovery of the ministry of healing in many churches, but any suggestion of the ministry of deliverance still makes many people extremely nervous.

I have a theory that not only is the actual content of Scripture important, but that even the proportions of Scripture are significant. That is to say, that if the Bible devotes a lot of space to a subject, that subject is important. If, on the other hand, a subject receives only a single, enigmatic mention, for example the millennium, it is not something to which we should devote very much of our attention. Now, in the gospels, for every two miracles of healing there is roughly one story of deliverance from evil spirits. If this proportion is significant then we should expect in our ministry to perform one deliverance for every two healings. Or, to put the matter another way, we should expect to encounter one person who is demonised for every two who are physically sick.

We had been slow in getting into the deliverance ministry at St Nicholas' and St George's. Developing a healing ministry is not easy. It requires a paradigm shift in our thinking, and it requires a new model for our practice. The same is true for the deliverance ministry, but they are even harder to make or to come by. Our Western scientific world-view finds it hard enough to accommodate the power of God to heal; it has rejected entirely the idea of demonisation. Few people in the main-stream churches seem prepared to teach or to demonstrate the ministry of deliverance. So it is difficult to gain any knowledge or experience except by trial and error, and there are plenty of disincentives to doing that.

There have been notorious cases of Christians erring only too grievously in this ministry, cases which have made the daily papers and brought the individuals concerned, the church at large, and the ministry of deliverance into disrepute. Who wants to be the next in line for that? As a result, the bishops of the Church of England, to which after all St George's and St Nicholas' belong, have set up a discipline which makes it difficult to do anything at all in the way of deliverance except after a long process of consultation and bureaucracy. It is called the Diocesan Deliverance Team.

My own early attempts to use the system (and I do believe in doing things according to the rules) had been frustrating. The frustration culminated in my being referred to a member of the bishop's Deliverance Team who informed me that he did not actually believe in evil spirits. At that point I wrote to the bishop himself to complain. He referred me to another member of the team who, he said, 'would be more sympathetic to my point of view'. In the end I was given permission to carry on by myself, with the Team as a sort of longstop if anything went wrong. That did not help very much in terms of equipping or training us, but at least I now felt I had proper authority to engage in this ministry myself. Perhaps in no other aspect of Christian ministry is it so important to do it right by the book, not only by *the* Book, but also by whatever book a particular church may have by way of discipline. I call it 'putting on the breastplate of righteousness'.

The initial problem with the deliverance ministry is knowing what is what. A person in the church has a particular set of symptoms. Are they physically ill? Are they traumatised? Or are they demonised? A person in a meeting starts to laugh uncontrollably. Is it the work of the Holy Spirit? Or is it the manifestation of a demon? I have never been able to discover any objective criteria by which one thing can be distinguished from another. Discernment is a gift of the Holy Spirit (1 Cor 12:10), and like other gifts of the Holy Spirit it is a subtle and delicate gift to receive and use.

The next difficulty is to introduce the possibility of demonisation to sufferers. Whatever most people think they have, it is not an evil spirit. The very idea can be shocking and horrifying. That is partly because it is understood that to have an evil spirit a person must be extremely wicked. A terrible burden of guilt can descend on anyone who conceives the idea that they may be demonised. Another misunderstanding is that this condition is especially dire: better to be terminally ill with cancer or a burnt-out schizophrenic than to be possessed by an evil spirit. So we have to be careful about how we talk to people, and how we pray with people, lest we fill them with unwarranted guilt or despair.

The fact is that while demonisation may be the result of personal sin, it is often the result of what has been done to us rather than what we have done ourselves. In any case, if it is our own fault the guilt can be washed away by the blood of Jesus like any other guilt. Secondly it is no more dire to have an evil spirit than to have back-ache or tummy-ache. In fact the two are not uncommonly related. It is no harder to receive deliverance than to receive healing, in the name of Jesus. Jesus has power over unclean spirits, just as he has power over infirmities and diseases. Being demonised is not a particularly big deal: it is troublesome, but doesn't have to be a big deal.

Vera had come to Maureen and me a couple of years before, to talk about her chronic and crippling fears. She had worked through with us various issues relating to the life and death of her father, and through our prayers together and the word of God in her life she had experienced a considerable measure of healing. But still a particular fear remained.

Some thirty years before, she and her husband Brian had lived in a semi-detached house with very noisy neighbours. This was not ordinary, happy, family noise, this was heavy rock music played at full volume, both out in the garden and through the party wall. Brian had complained and also tried to reason with these neighbours, but this was a form of deliberate persecution. Day and night, in sickness and in health, Vera never knew when the terrible blast of sound would suddenly hit her again. She began to spend whole days away from the house, to dread going home, and to dread going out into the garden. Finally she and Brian moved away. But Vera took the fear with her.

Over the years of their married life they had now moved thirteen times. Irrespective of who their new neighbours were or what they were like, Vera's fears always returned. She could neither stay in one house nor find any relief in another. She had consulted doctors and psychiatrists but all they could do was prescribe tranquillisers.

One day during the ministry of the Holy Spirit Vera came forward to seek specific prayer for this fear. She fell down under the power of the Spirit and felt something moving up from her stomach, into her chest and then into her throat. But there it seemed to disappear. Nothing came out. After a while we decided to close the ministry down for the time being and see Vera privately on another occasion. We assured her that she would be well one day, and made a date to visit her at home.

A few days later Maureen and I were able to find out more from Vera and Brian about the nature of this affliction. It had recently become worse again. Every morning as Vera woke up her stomach turned over with fear. She had to pray hard and pluck up all her courage even to put the washing out on the line. If she went out in the car she did not know how to face the return home. All the time her bowels were in turmoil and she suffered with almost permanent diarrhoea. Her life was a misery. 'I feel as if I am possessed,' she said.

It was not difficult by now to agree that that was the correct diagnosis. Reassuring her again, we prayed, this time more explicitly, that the unclean spirit would come out of her. We spoke to it in Jesus' name. Once more something started to move upwards from her stomach, into her chest and then into her throat – where once more it seemed to disappear and nothing came out. Vera could tell us what was going on, and she cooperated herself, calling on the name of Jesus. Once again however, we had to leave the ministry with a sense that it was still uncompleted. Each time Vera felt better for a few days afterwards, but before long the fear returned.

Peter Lawrence says that anyone who has ever put a child to bed can drive out evil spirits; they may not go the first time you tell them, but they go in the end. So some weeks later we arranged to meet Vera again, this time on her own but in the church. We kept her sitting on a chair as, once again, we commanded the spirit to come out and leave her. The same movement began, from the stomach, up through the chest, into the throat. This time I was determined that we should not lose it. I recalled that I had read somewhere that a spirit had to leave by the same way that it came in. So I now commanded it to come out through the ears. At that moment Vera suddenly felt a sharp pain in her left ear, and the spirit came out. She knew at once it had gone.

For several days afterwards Vera had the sensation that something foul was coming out of her mouth. It was not a frightening sensation; she was glad it was going. It was not a material substance that came out, but a sensation of something unseen being evacuated. Her stomach also rumbled a great deal, as if it were settling down happily after years of upheaval. Vera was free.

—

SEVENTEEN

TO DIE IS GAIN

As part of our attempts to learn about the ministry of deliverance we had invited a Nigerian priest, who was staying in Britain but who had extensive experience of this type of ministry in his own country, to come over and spend a day with us ministering to some of our hard cases. These were people with whom we had prayed in various ways in the past without apparently much success. It was interesting that Bill did not seem to have very much more success than we had done, but in the process we did learn a lot about the ministry of deliverance.

However, it was on this day that I myself was taken mysteriously ill. This illness was to threaten my life and bring me close to God in a new way. I do not understand what the spiritual connection was between the day of deliverance and my illness, but some connection there seemed to be.

The day of Bill's visit I woke up in the morning with slightly aching limbs. By mid-day I was sure I had 'flu, and felt ill enough to excuse myself from the afternoon session and leave the ministry to Bill and the others. I went to bed, not unduly worried. But the following morning I was feeling worse, and by ten o'clock I was juddering with a high fever.

At this point there began a series of extraordinary coincidences which were to reassure me that God was with me throughout these bizarre events. Unable to contact our own doctor, we rang for an ambulance. Amazingly, an ambulance was already in our village and in less than two minutes it was standing at the door. The ambulanceman who came up the stairs had recently attended our Alpha course. Two or three people, including the ambulanceman, stood round the bed and prayed for me before deciding to take me into hospital.

The journey to our nearest general hospital took three-quarters of an hour, during which time I began to vomit. However, after an examination in Casualty Ward I was fixed up with some antibiotic tablets and sent home again. My symptoms, far from abating, became worse and worse. I vomited the antibiotics and everything else I took, including water. My fever raged on. It was the hottest weekend of the year and I was rapidly dehydrating. The third morning our own doctor visited and declared that I should never have been discharged the previous day, that I must go straight back into hospital.

On their first visit, the ambulance crew had managed to leave behind in the rectory a black case. Maureen, having brought the case to the hospital when she fetched me that day, was asked to deliver it to the ambulance station on the way home. But the ambulance station was deserted and locked up, so we had to bring the case back to the rectory again. On the morning of the doctor's visit, the ambulance station had rung to enquire about the case and to arrange to collect it that morning. Imagine the doctor's astonishment when she telephoned for the ambulance to come: she had not replaced the receiver before the door bell rang, and the ambulance had arrived. She knew that the ambulance service was trying to improve its response time, but this was ridiculous! Imagine the astonishment of the ambulance crew too: as they drew up at the rectory to collect their case a message came over their radio to collect their next patient, from the same address. 'We're there now,' they told their control centre.

For the second time in twenty-four hours I was on my way to hospital. This time I knew I was seriously ill. Something deep inside me told me that unless my body got help from outside, I was going to die. I was still vomiting bile at regular intervals. My mouth and my eyes were now completely dry. I faced the possibility of death.

I have always had an instinctive fear of death. As my faith has become stronger, and especially since I was filled with the Holy Spirit, I have been less afraid. But at that point, as the ambulance trundled interminably along the country lanes, I was afraid again. I collected my wits. I prayed:

'Heavenly Father, I ask you to forgive me all the sins I have ever committed, known and unknown, for Jesus' sake.
Father, I now forgive all those who have ever sinned against me, known and unknown, for Jesus' sake.
Father, I ask you to receive me into your kingdom in heaven, for Jesus' sake.'

Fear left me. I knew I was ready to die. I was at peace in the hands of God whatever the outcome.

This time I was admitted to the hospital proper. Blood tests were taken, I was put on an intravenous drip to rehydrate me. I had contracted septicaemia. I was put on a course of intravenous antibiotics. I did not die. In a few days I was able to go home. It was several weeks before I returned to work, and several months before I felt fully fit again.

During that time I was put through a series of tests and examinations to try to determine how and why I should have developed septicaemia. After feeling my stomach all over on yet another occasion, the doctor murmured, 'No, there is no mass there'. With another jolt I realised that they were examining me for cancer. For the next few months I went backwards and forwards to hospital not knowing what the news would be. I realised the sort of pressures people experience at such times, the uncertainty, the sudden foreshortening of the horizon.

During this time I found immeasurable strength and help in Philippians 1:19-26:

> Yes, and I will continue to rejoice, for I know that through your prayers and the help given by the Spirit of Jesus Christ, what has happened to me will turn out for my deliverance. I eagerly expect and hope that I will in no way be ashamed, but will have sufficient courage so that now as always Christ will be exalted in my body, whether by life or by death. For to me, to live is Christ and to die is gain. If I am to go on living in the body, this will mean fruitful labour for me. Yet what shall I choose? I do not know! I am torn between the two: I desire to depart and be with Christ, which is better by far; but it is more necessary for you that I remain in the body. Convinced of this, I know that I will remain, and I will continue with all of you for your progress and joy in the faith so that through my being with you again your joy in Christ Jesus will overflow on account of me.

I did feel sure that it was necessary for me to remain in the body for the sake of the progress and joy in the faith of those to whom I had been ministering these last six years. I did feel that my work was not yet done. But I did also know then that while I might go on living in the body, and that that would mean fruitful labour, it would be far better to depart and be with Christ. To live might be Christ, but to die would be gain.

I did live. Every test drew a blank. At the end of three months the doctors simply had to admit that they did not know why I had been taken so ill so suddenly. Nothing was constitutionally wrong with me.

The whole episode remains a mystery, to the doctors and to me. Why did God permit me to be attacked in such a manner? He was so manifestly in charge of every incidence in those few days, but I still do not understand what was going on. I count it all a blessing, but what a strange blessing.

I know that I have been within sight of the gates of death. I know that I shall one day go that way again, and not come back, but go on through them to the other side. I have lost my fear of that awful road. I know that the Good Shepherd does go with us to comfort us. I can pray and talk more easily now with others who are treading that same path.

I also know that God uses the National Health Service. When I was sweating out a fever of over 104° I prayed every sort of prayer I could think of for my own healing, and others prayed for me too. I prayed the prayer of faith; I stood on the promise of God; I claimed my healing; I came against the powers of the enemy; I rebuked sickness in the name of Jesus. There was no miraculous intervention of the power of God, just the normal provision of doctors, ambulances, antibiotics and intravenous drips. That was the way God healed me. It was no less real as an answer to prayer.

Perhaps I learned above all a new level of trust in God. We are to love him for himself alone, not for what he can give or do for us. We are to trust him even when we do not understand what is going on. Is there any way for these things to become real, except by some such route as God caused me to travel?

> Though the fig-tree does not bud and there are no grapes on the vines, though the olive crop fails and the fields produce no food, though there are no sheep in the pen and no cattle in the stalls, yet I will rejoice in the Lord, I will be joyful in God my Saviour (Hab 3:17-18).

God is faithful, but he is not predictable. Or perhaps I should put it the other way round: God is not predictable, but he is faithful. Even though it is not always obvious to us, God is good, and God knows what he is doing.

—

EIGHTEEN

THE LORD WILL DO WHAT IS GOOD IN HIS SIGHT

At the age of nine Jean had German measles and glandular fever in quick succession. When she recovered she was partially crippled. Somehow the nervous system in the lower part of her body had been damaged. She was unable to walk with a normal gait. As the years went by she had to resort to sticks, then to crutches.

From the beginning her mother had treated her with prayer as well as medicine. Jean had been taken to specialists in South Africa, Canada and Britain to try to find a cure. As an adult Christian she had herself sought healing from God, not only in her own prayers, but at healing services, Christian healing centres and conventions. Over and over again she had received the laying on of hands. Her condition remained the same.

Now, some fifty years on, she and her husband Alan had moved into our area in retirement and joined the congregation at St Nicholas'. Another group of Christians began to encourage and exhort her to seek the healing touch of God. On many occasions we laid hands on her and prayed for her spiritual, mental and physical wholeness. Jean continued to read books about Christian healing and went on hoping. Still her condition did not improve. What were we to say about Jean, and more particularly, what were we to say *to* Jean?

The theology and practice of the healing ministry pose a real problem. If we start from the Bible, we see that Jesus healed the sick. It was a major part of his ministry. Miracles of healing were the commonest of the signs and wonders which authenticated the gospel message which he preached. Moreover, emphasis is laid upon the fact that he healed all kinds of diseases and infirmities (Matt 9:35), and that he healed all who came to him (Lk 4:40). He did not indeed heal every sick person he ever saw or passed in the street. At the pool of Bethesda he picked out just one cripple from a multitude of disabled people, and healed him alone (Jn 5:1-9). But in this case Jesus had gone to him; he had not gone to Jesus. It is an important distinction.

Sometimes, as at the pool of Bethesda, Jesus took the initiative. Another example is the man born blind (Jn 9:1). In these cases Jesus was no doubt responding to a direct prompting of the Holy Spirit. The Father revealed to the Son what he was going to do, and the Son worked with the Father to do it. But on many other occasions the sick came to Jesus to be healed; the initiative was theirs. Then, the gospel record is clear: he healed them all.

Those who came had faith. Jesus often says to them 'Your faith has healed you' (Lk 8:48). The faith that they had was not some special degree of inward conviction. The man with the epileptic boy could only confess his unbelief (Mk 9:24). The faith was in the coming.

We never read of Jesus saying to a sick person, 'I am sorry, your particular disease is incurable. Some diseases I can heal, but not yours.' He healed every disease and every infirmity. We never read of Jesus saying to a sick person, 'I am sorry, it is not God's will to heal you. Others, the Father and I will heal, but not you. You must bear your sickness.' He healed all who came to him. Again, we never read of Jesus saying to any sick person who came to him, 'I am sorry, you do not have enough faith. I can only heal those who have great faith, not people of little faith like you.' The faith to come was all that Jesus required.

This is the ministry which Jesus entrusted to his disciples. Sending out the Twelve and the seventy-two he said, 'Heal the sick' (Matt 10:8, Lk 10:9). The apostles continued to heal the sick after the resurrection. Again, some emphasis is laid on the fact that all who were brought and all who came were healed (Acts 5:16).

This is both confirmation and demonstration that the perfect will of God is always for our healing and wholeness. There was no sickness or disease in God's original creation. When God had finished his creative work he declared that everything was very good (Gen 1:31). No sickness or disease there then. Likewise in the new heaven and the new earth, when the work of redemption is complete, there will be 'no more death or mourning or crying or pain' (Rev 21:4). No sickness or disease there then either. Disease and infirmity belong to our present, intermediate, fallen state: a state in which 'the whole world is under the control of the evil one' (1 Jn 5:19). Sickness is one of the works of the enemy who comes only 'to steal and kill and destroy' (Jn 10:10). Thus it is one of the principle things from which Jesus came to deliver us and set us free. Jesus announces that the Kingdom, the rule of God, is at hand, and he demonstrates the reality of it by healing the sick.

As the followers of Jesus, we are commissioned to preach the same gospel and to do the same works as he did (Jn 14:12). As Jesus instructed us, we lay hands on the sick with the expectation that they will recover (Mk 16:18). And sometimes they do. It still works. The sick are healed as we step out in faith and obedience. But not all. There are the Jeans, who are not healed, or at least not healed at once. What are we to say about them, and more particularly what are we to say *to* them?

There is a gap between our faith and our experience, between our theology and our practice. It is as well to admit the gap; no good is done by pretending it does not exist. Some people try to eliminate the gap. Some would change the theology. But I do not believe that this can be done without a denial or distortion of some part of the biblical witness. Others would change the terms of the practice. If people are not healed, they themselves must be to blame: they have some blockage which prevents them from receiving their healing. There may be some elements of truth in this, but we have to acknowledge that the people who came to Jesus must have had the same blockages as we do. Jesus identified and removed them.

Both Scripture, modern medicine, and everyday experience confirm that there are subtle connections between body, mind, and spirit. There are connections between sicknesses of the body, sicknesses of the mind, and sicknesses of the spirit. Healing undoubtedly depends on finding the root of the problem, whatever that may be. Jesus was able to do this unerringly. He perceived that, in the case of one man who was brought to him, the root of his paralysis was guilt. So he said to him, 'Your sins are forgiven' (Matt 9:12). Another woman was bent double and could not straighten herself up. Jesus discerned that the root of her problem was demonic. He delivered her from the evil spirit and she was able to stand upright. In other cases, like that of blind Bartimaeus, the problem was purely physical, and Jesus healed him with a word or a touch.

We are probably not as good as Jesus was at discerning what is at the root of peoples' problems. There may be times when we are trying to deal with somebody's physical symptoms, when the real problem is one of unconfessed or unrepented sin. We may be praying for healing when what a person actually needs is deliverance or, on the contrary, we may be trying to deliver someone from an evil spirit whose need is really for emotional healing. It all depends on knowing what we ought to be doing, and that is not easy: the symptoms are often confusingly alike.

Again, despite the promise of Jesus that those who believe in him will do even greater works than he did (Jn 14:12), there is a hint in the gospels that disciples can be less effective than their master. When Jesus came down from the mountain after the transfiguration he found a boy possessed by an evil spirit, and his disciples in some confusion. Jesus cast the spirit out, but the disciples had not been able to do so.

All this suggests that if we are to seek a reason for the gap between our theology and our practise in the ministry of healing, we should look for it in the deficiency of the ministers not in the deficiencies of the sick. Too often we are tempted to turn our failures back upon the poor creatures who are already suffering. Many sick people like Jean have been told, 'You do not have enough faith', or 'You have some hidden sin in your life', or 'You must be keeping a door open to a demon'. This may seem to excuse the minister's failure. But Jesus never said such things to anyone. It is better to say to such a person as Jean, 'I am sorry that we have not been able to help you'. She has come in faith. If she goes away unhealed, it is more our failure than hers.

God permitted Job to suffer as a test of his faith; a test which Job seems on the whole to have failed. God allowed Paul to continue to be afflicted by a thorn in the flesh in order to prevent him from becoming too conceited (2 Cor 12:7). I believe that people like Jean can be strengthened by the example of Job: not indeed in seeing their disease as sent or willed by God, but in seeing it as a challenge to maintain their trust in him even though they are not healed. I also believe that people like Jean can be strengthened by the word which God spoke to Paul, 'My grace is sufficient for you' (2 Cor 12:9).

In the end folklore is wrong; the most important thing in life is not health; it is God. There is a fate worse than death; it is to live and die without God. Much better to be on crutches and know the grace of God, like Jean, than to be a top-class athlete and be lost for ever. Knowing Jesus involves a radical change in our values. He is the precious pearl which is more valuable than everything else put together, even more valuable than health or life itself. And how is that to be real to us except through some such experience as Jean's?

The problem for Jean is to maintain a belief that God both can heal her and might heal her in the face of her experience so far. Jean has known times of expectation, occasions when she has anticipated that she would be healed. Then she has known times of depression when those immediate expectations were disappointed. It is only too easy for those of us who are well to be critical and judgemental. Jean has had to learn not to strive. She has come to God in the only way she can, as she is. God requires no more. She has asked in faith. All she can do now is say with Joab, 'The Lord will do what is good in his sight' (1 Chron 19:13). Ultimately we have to acknowledge the sovereignty of God

—

NINETEEN

LIVING WATER

'I want something bigger.'

It was one of those occasions when I suspected that God was talking to me. We had just organised a conference in our cathedral city on the ministry of prophecy. An American pastor from Kansas City had been the guest speaker and about two hundred people had turned up. It was an encouraging response, and at the end of the conference, as we were worshipping God and praying for an increase of the prophetic anointing on the Church, I thought I heard God say, 'I want something bigger'.

I was wary. I had come across too many examples of Christian megalomania not to be wary of falling into the same trap: little, insignificant churches which think God has big plans for them. Too often it is merely the wishful thinking of the flesh disguised in biblical quotations.

One of the first ways of testing prophetic words is to lay them before other people. So bit by bit I tried the idea out on other Christians. What God seemed to me to be talking about was a three-day-event, held over a Bank Holiday weekend, Saturday, Sunday, and Monday. Our two churches had benefited so much from people going away to Christian family conferences in other places. Above all we had taken a party each year to *New Wine* in Somerset, a party which had grown over the years from nine to sixty. Many individual lives had been changed during these weeks, but the experience we had shared together had also helped to change our churches.

Nothing like *New Wine* however took place in our part of the country. Indeed it often seemed as if nothing took place in our part of the country. Sparsely populated, with a multitude of villages and few large towns, we did not seem to be on the circuit for big Christian events. Consequently very few people knew about such happenings, let alone went to them. You have to be fairly committed already to travel over 250 miles, use up a week's annual holiday, and live in a tent with only cold showers for comfort, simply in order to worship God. Even in our own congregations there were many people who had never been to *New Wine*, older people put off by the journey, wives with unsaved husbands, people who simply could not take a week off at that time of year.

A three-day event in our own region seemed to be what God wanted. People who lived within fifty miles or so could travel in daily, sleep in their own beds, and wash in their own bathrooms. No one would have to take annual leave. This event might be able to reach parts of the church which other Christian events were not reaching.

As I talked about it to other people, the idea began to catch on. We had a fine agricultural showground in Norfolk which would make an ideal venue. I enquired: yes, it would be available on the first Bank Holiday weekend in May; yes, we could hire it.

What about money? Robbie, ignorant of these tentative plans, rang up one day about her two sons. Identical twins, they had grown up and become Christians at St

Nicholas'. Now living away they had well-paid jobs as actuaries. Still young and unmarried they were looking for some Christian project to which to give money over and above their own local church. Had I any suggestions? I had. This obviously would not be enough to fund the whole event, but it would prime the pump. It was as if God was saying to me, 'You put on the event, I will provide the money'.

Next we needed an administrator. I was aware that we could not organise an event of this sort without extra help. Becky had also grown up at St Nicholas'. She herself had had a life-changing experience of God at *New Wine*. She was now a student doing a degree in Business Studies. As part of her course she had had to do a year of practical work, and she had done it in the *New Wine* office. Now, recently married to John, a local boy, Becky was looking for a job which would use her expertise and experience. 'If you like, I'll be your administrator'.

Only God can do things like that. By now I was certain that God was in this, and had had it all planned out for us long before. One snag remained. Youth for Christ, who had for many years held their own May-Day event in the same city, attracted a large crowd of all ages. It could not be right to run another event a few miles away on the same weekend. I contacted Ian, the director of Youth for Christ, and I shared with him our vision. Their thoughts had also been tentatively moving in the direction of something bigger, but they had been inhibited up to then by their lack of extra resources. Our visions coalesced, and from then on we worked together to produce our own regional event, *Living Water*.

It was a huge operation which dwarfed anything I had ever been involved in before. The budget came close to £100,000. We needed a team of 250 people to run the event itself and to staff the programmes for all the different age groups. If God had not been in it, the event would never have taken place. There was no way in which I could have recruited such a team and enthused them for the work. But so many people caught the vision, offered to help, recruited others, gave their time and energy willingly and sacrificially, that it was no effort at all for me.

At the end of nearly two years of planning the week of *Living Water* arrived. The office moved onto the Showground. Contractors started to arrive on site to put up tents, install toilets and showers, up-rate the electricity supply, convert farm-buildings into venues for worship and teaching. The Sheep Building, appropriately, became the auditorium for the adults; carpets were laid, chairs set out, light and sound systems installed, a stage erected, banners raised. Throughout the week the sun shone as if it were mid-summer instead of early May. God was smiling.

The day before the event, cars started to drive in; people registered, pitched their tents and caravans; the site began to fill up and come alive. Ian and Maureen and I went round and prayed with each team, that God would come by his Spirit, bless their work, and use them to change the lives of adults, teenagers, and children.

Finally the day dawned. In the adult pavilion the seats filled up, the lights came on; we welcomed the people, about a quarter of whom were at an event of this sort for the very first time. The band struck up and we began to worship God:

> Down the mountain the river flows
> And it brings refreshing wherever it goes
> Through the valley and over the fields
> The river is rushing and the river is here.
> (*The river is here*, Andy Park)

God came, and God blessed the event more than we could ask or think. One teenager wrote afterwards:

I just wanted to write to tell you that while I was at *Living Water* God healed my anorexia. He did it very gently, step by step. I went to *Living Water* having decided that I didn't want any more to do with God. On the first day I didn't go forward for prayer but one of the team came to talk to me. Amazingly she was the woman doing the talk on eating disorders. She prayed that I wouldn't be scared to open myself completely to God and let him take over. In the evening I did go forward and I said to God, 'God I give up!'. From then on he took over. While on the floor he sorted out a lot of things that I thought I'd dealt with but obviously hadn't. The next time I was on the floor and I felt like someone was punching me in the stomach and knocking all the wind out of me – God was knocking all the bad stuff out, the anorexia and all that. It carried on all night, so that even when I was walking around I kept jerking forward. The next day, when I was prayed for, the same thing happened, only this time God was filling up all the gaps that had been left by the anorexia with himself. Anorexia had been the centre of my life – everything – for so long. Now God is in it's place, so there's no room for it anymore. I spent the rest of the weekend celebrating. Now I just want the world to know what God has done for me.

TWENTY

—

TEACH OTHERS

Marshall McLuhan wrote, 'The medium is the message'. This gnomic remark can be taken in various ways. At one level it means that in our society the mass-media are not only channels by which messages reach us but they are themselves now part of the message. Thus, the nightly television news features reports on events happening around the world, but the news bulletin itself is an event; what is reported on it and the way it is reported is itself significant, and influences the course of other events.

This is true in the world of Christian literature as much as anywhere else. I wrote a book called *Speak to These Bones* which described what God had done in our two small country churches, St Nicholas' and St George's. But that book then became a significant part of the life of these two churches. *Speak to These Bones* was the foundation on which *Living Water* was built. As one of the hosts of *Living Water*, I was identified as the author of that book.

The book also led to a series of conferences in which I was able to share with other church leaders some of the lessons I had learned in the process of leading a traditional church into renewal. The spiritual renewal of the churches has progressed much further and much faster in some parts of Britain than in others. On the whole it has progressed least in the rural areas. That is not because there are no renewed Christians or even no renewed clergy in the villages, but it is because there are certain constraints and blockages which make renewal in such circumstances more difficult. The opportunity to speak at and organise conferences on this subject arose directly out of the book. And it was the exercise of writing the book that caused me to analyse the process which we had been through.

The chief constraint in country towns and villages is that there is virtually nowhere else for people to go. In a larger town or city there are probably a considerable number of churches of different denominations, traditions and churchmanship. If one church decides to embrace the charismatic option, then renewed Christians gravitate towards that church and others gravitate out. There may be some personal pain involved, but large numbers of people are not being unchurched. That is how churches work nowadays. Anglican parish boundaries are virtually meaningless in suburbs and cities; people ride in their cars to the churches of their choice.

Not so much in rural areas. Although such eclectic congregations are becoming increasingly common, a country church is likely to contain Christians of many different backgrounds and even denominations. Those with an explicitly sectarian doctrine of the church may opt to worship outside their own community, but most will want to stay in if they can. A country parish church is a community church in a much more demanding and difficult sense than many a new church with that name in town.

How is a leader to lead such a community church into renewal?

First, the leader must actually renounce the idea that the situation urges upon him, that it is his job to keep everyone happy. I know more than one clergyman who has had a nervous breakdown trying to keep everyone happy. We are simply not called to keep everyone happy: we are called to make God happy. The test of our ministry is not whether our parishioners are happy with it, but whether God is happy with it. So, the question a leader must settle with himself is, what does God want the church to be like? Who wants renewal in the church?

Perhaps the leader himself wants renewal. That alone is not a sufficient reason to introduce it. After all, the church is not some private fief where I can have things my own way. And it will not be a sufficient reason in particular when the going gets tough. A leader may want to see the church renewed, but when it comes to the crunch most of us would prefer a quiet life.

Perhaps the people in the congregation want renewal in the church, or at least some of them do. That is fine. But there will almost certainly be others who want to keep things just as they are. Which of the two or three or more parties in the church should the leader back? Too often he tries to back them all or none, and ends up having a nervous breakdown.

What does God want? That is all that matters, and it is the one question to which the church leader must know the answer. If the present renewal is the work of God in our generation, then that is the way we must go. As the people of Israel journeyed through the wilderness on their way to the Promised Land they were led by a pillar of cloud by day and of fire by night. When the pillar stopped, they stopped and pitched their tents. When the pillar moved on, they had to pack up and move on. Sometimes the stops were short, sometimes longer. Sometimes they stopped in pleasant places, sometimes less pleasant. But when God moved on, they had to follow. It is still the same today. It is especially the leader's job to see where God is going, and lead the people in the same direction.

Encouraged and taught and led, some people in the church will be willing to follow. Others will refuse. That is the nature of leading a traditional church into renewal. There will be some sort of a tug-of-war between the people who want to move on and the people who want to stand still. I know of no traditional church that has come into renewal where this has not been true. At this point the leader needs to have a strategy for dealing with the situation. There are three possibilities: fight, compromise or separate.

One strategy is mortal combat, fight to the death. The leader and his supporters battle away until the opposition is beaten from the field or is, quite literally, dead (from natural causes of course). This may take years. There will be blood on the vestry carpet and on the streets. It will not be a happy or a quiet life while it is going on. It will not do the name of the church any good in the community at large, especially in a village. But some people may be called to do it that way.

The second strategy is compromise. This sounds the more Christian way. But it is in fact a snare and a delusion. It is a recipe for frustration and inertia. Far from being the way to keep everyone happy, it is the way to keep everyone unhappy: the traditionalists feel constantly threatened by change and the people who want renewal feel constantly frustrated by the need to appease the traditionalists. We tried this way, explicitly at St George's. It does not work. I now believe in separation.

This strategy means that the traditional church goes on; the traditionalists are not threatened with change at all. But somewhere else, at some other time we can grow a new church alongside the old. The new church may have to start in the week, in the church hall or in someone's home. As it grows it can assume a higher profile and, sooner or later, find a slot in the Sunday schedule. But it does not have to compromise. There, God can be God. We can take and use anything from the old tradition that may be useful, but we can also be free to learn the new things that God is doing, the new ways of worship, the new ways of ministry in the power of the Spirit. Jesus said, 'Every teacher of the law who has been instructed about the kingdom of heaven is like the owner of a house who brings out of his storeroom new treasures as well as old' (Matt 13:52). That is a motto for anyone leading a traditional church into renewal, and growing a new church alongside an old one.

The history of the church may then follow one of two or three courses. First, and ideally, the old church and the new one will coalesce again. This will happen if all the people in the traditional church voluntarily come over into the renewed one. It happens with individuals as God touches them and opens them up to himself. It is more likely to happen where people are given the freedom to choose without pressure or coercion. But it is unusual; it is unusual for all the traditionalists to change.

Secondly, and more commonly, the two churches will go on side by side, either in total isolation from one another, or with an area of overlap. The overlap consists of the people from either side who want to build bridges or keep bridges open. Whatever we intended to do or thought we were doing at St George's and St Nicholas', this is the situation with which we actually ended up. In both churches we have virtually two congregations, a renewed one and a traditional one, with a small area of overlap between.

Separation may not seem ideal from the Christian point of view. Are we not supposed to glorify God with one heart and one voice? But separation is better than fighting. When the herdsmen of Abram started to fight the herdsmen of Lot over who should use the wells to water their flocks, Abram and Lot decided to separate, and they went their separate ways (Gen 13:8-9).

So I now say, separate and let God be the judge. Let the traditional church and the renewed church co-exist side by side. Let the leader minister to both, and see which one God blesses. No one comes to Jesus at all unless the Father draws him (Jn 6:44). People saw at one time that the congregation around John the Baptist was declining while the congregation around Jesus was increasing. But John replied, 'A man can only receive what is given him from heaven' (Jn 3:27). Separate, and see which congregation increases. See where God chooses to draw people to Jesus. When Jacob was keeping Laban's flocks, Laban repeatedly tried to manipulate the blessing of God, but without success. If Laban said the speckled ones should be Jacob's wages then all the flock bore speckled; but if he said the streaked ones should be his wages all the flock bore streaked (Gen 31:8). Let God decide which flock to bless.

—

TWENTY-ONE

FREELY GIVE

The mission statement of the Toronto Airport Vineyard is: 'To walk in God's love and give it away'. Without having defined it as our aim, we found that we were involved in doing the same thing.

Fiona lived in a village nearly ten miles away. She was a friend of Louise who lived in one of our villages. Through Louise, Fi came to know Jesus and started to travel over to church at St Nicholas'. In her own village the services were irregular, and even when there was a service it was rarely suitable for children. So Fi brought Athena and later Luke to the morning service and Sunday school in our village. One Sunday her husband Tim came too. That morning Tim had a life-changing encounter with God. Now there were four. Next, Fi's mother, who lived in the same village as Fi, also started to come: five. Tim was talking to a young man with whom he worked; Dave became a Christian too: six. None of them lived in our villages.

Bill and Pat retired and came to live in another village about three miles from us. They had both been converted in middle-age and had joined a Baptist church near their previous home. Now they were looking for a place to worship in their new area. The Anglican church in their own village was about a mile away, and was emphatically traditional. Bill and Pat shopped around for six months. They visited and worshipped at a number of different fellowships within a radius of several miles, before finally deciding that they felt most at home at St Nicholas'. So they joined us.

We had first noticed that people were coming to our two churches from outside the parish some two years before. Strangers are noticed in a village church. We had always made people welcome without ever looking for recruits outside our own two parishes. But God was sending them to us. Some, like Tim and Fi, were converted through the ministry of our churches. Others, like Bill and Pat, moved into the area without pre-existing links with any other church and found their way to us. Others came too: Christians from other villages who were looking for more than their own churches were providing. One way or another they heard that God was among us, and came over to St George's or St Nicholas'. Some came on occasional visits; others came and stayed.

For several years we had been holding an informal service on a Saturday evening, with an extended time of praise and worship, a ministry of the Word and of the Spirit. Originally this had been a time for our own two congregations to meet together and grow in the things of the Spirit. Much of what we had learned and introduced there had found its way into the ordinary Sunday services and we then found our own people coming less on Saturday nights. But at the same time others began to come from outside. Soon there were groups coming from ten, twenty, even fifty miles away. Month by month the numbers crept up, until we began to wonder where we were going to put them all.

When we started the Alpha course we only had our own congregations and parishioners in mind. But from the outset we found that we had as many people from outside the parishes as from inside. Our own people had done as they were told: they had invited their friends and relations to come to Alpha. The only trouble was, they had friends and relations who lived in other parishes.

That's life! Or, that's life at the end of the twentieth century. People just do not live their lives within neat parish boundaries any more. Villages are still distinct communities, but the village is only one community amongst many to which people belong. The community of the family extends across many towns and villages. The community of friends spreads across an equally large area. The community of work is unlikely to be within the village, but may be situated many miles away, and draw people together from dozens of different places. Even the communities of schools usually draw children from more than one parish. The connections that people have are the product of many factors, only one of which is the place where they live.

The life of the Church of England, especially in the countryside, however, is based on a different presumption. The presumption is that whatever else people may do outside their own parish, go to work, go to school, shop, visit the doctor, the dentist, the bank, even the Post Office and the pubs, they will or ought to worship at their own parish church. Unfortunately for the parish system of the Church of England, it does not work like that as it used to. Some people go out of the village to worship; Roman Catholics, Pentecostals, and sundry others go out for denominational reasons. Some Anglicans, who do not like our style of worship, go out of the parish in search of a style they do like. And Anglicans and people of other denominations now travel in to our parishes because they are finding something there that they do not find at home. Old villagers tend to stick to their own church or go to none. But the rest, the new arrivals and the younger generation of villagers more used to mobility, these worship, as they do everything else, wherever they like.

Some in the Church of England find this difficult to understand or accept. Sometimes, maintaining the parish system seems to be more important than building up the kingdom of God. A whiff of disapproval surrounds people travelling out of the parish to worship, even if it means people being added to the Kingdom of God, and even to the Church of England. 'Magnet-churches', like ours had become, are not popular with the hierarchy or with surrounding parishes. But our own Parochial Church Councils began to find the situation worrying too.

This anxiety surfaced one night at a meeting of St Nicholas' PCC. 'We seem to have more and more people coming to our church from outside the parish. We don't want them taking the church over, or taking it away from our own villagers. And what happens if all these strangers leave again? They could be here today and gone tomorrow.' I looked round at the twenty or so members of the Church Council. Every single one of them lived in the parish. Nobody seemed to be taking over from us. The church was still there for any of our own villagers who cared to attend. The simple fact was that most of them did not, whatever sort of services we had, and whether people came from outside the parish or not. There were still spare seats if the villagers wanted to sit in them. Besides, what could we say to people who arrived from other parishes? Jesus said, 'Whoever comes to me I will never drive away' (Jn 5:37). Were we to say something different? Were we to drive people away?

Another question arose over the *Living Water* event. This did not take place in our own parishes at all, and it was meant for a much wider audience altogether. It involved a tremendous amount of work and an army of helpers. Murmurings were heard in St George's, 'We pay our diocesan quota in order to have a rector of our own. We don't pay for a rector running off here, there and everywhere. It stands to reason, if he is doing all these other things, he is not doing his job in this parish.' This was a bit hard. Not long before, I had declined to serve as Rural Dean in our area, and the bishop had mildly questioned my commitment to the wider church. Now people were questioning my commitment to my own churches. But of course it was a real question.

I tried to explain that the wider ministry of *Living Water* was not just mine, but ours, our two churches'. Without them it would have been nothing; it simply would not have happened. Of course our two churches had not run the event on their own. We had depended heavily on Youth for Christ and volunteers from many other churches as well. Even then, many of the key workers, from the full-time administrator downwards, were members of our two churches, and dozens of people from our two congregations had given themselves, body and soul, to making the event a success. *Living Water* was not just me; it was us, ministering to others on a large scale.

Not only that, but I was also aware that my own credibility depended on the life of these two churches. I might set up conferences about leading a traditional church into renewal, but the only recommendation I had for speaking on this subject lay in St George's and St Nicholas'. Like the church of Corinth for Paul, these churches were my only letter of recommendation (2 Cor 3:2). Apart from these two churches I would only be another theoretician.

I had no qualification to teach others, except our shared experience.

The first generation of leaders in the charismatic movement had been men with exceptional spiritual giftings. They had generally been raised up in local churches, but then taken up itinerant ministries. The pattern had changed now. God seemed to be raising up, not so much gifted individuals, but strong churches which could share what God had given them with others. I was not in the mould of the gifted charismatic evangelist or healer. I was nothing outside these two churches which God had given me to pastor. My ministry was to them: any wider ministry was ours, not mine alone.

The question was: how wide was our corporate vision? We certainly had a ministry to our own villages and nobody was suggesting that we should neglect that. But could we see that we might have a ministry to others beyond the confines of our parish boundaries; to those who might come hungry to our tables from other villages round about; to other churches and their leaders who might want to follow the path we had trodden; to those from further away who might catch a glimpse of a new relationship with God, a new meaning in worship, and a new power to change their lives, at an event like *Living Water*? It is one thing to walk in the love of God, another to give it away.

—

TWENTY-TWO

BE SHEPHERDS

'Receive the Holy Spirit...'

The bishop laid his hands on Alan's head as he said these words in the act of ordination.

The Church of England preserves three orders of ministry, all of which can claim to be Scriptural, even though they may now be practised in somewhat curious and distorted ways. Bishops continue to fulfil, in a recognisable form, the apostolic function of oversight of a number of local churches. But the office of deacon, to which, on this first occasion, Alan was being ordained, is now no more than a probationary year for someone on the way to becoming a priest or presbyter. If it is the office of those appointed to look after matters of church administration in Acts 6:1-6, then we do have deacons in the Church of England, but they are actually churchwardens, treasurers, parish administrators and fabric officers. At the moment we mock the office of deacon at ordination.

The office of priest or presbyter is the Scriptural office of elder. The trouble is that whereas in the Bible there are several elders in each church, in the Anglican Church in the countryside today there are several churches to each elder. This distorts the relationship of elders to churches completely. Part of the problem has been financial. At least since the nineteenth century the clergy of the Church of England have been seen as a professional élite. To return to a more biblical pattern we have to begin by deprofessionalising the office of elder. The Church of England has been moving in this direction for about twenty-five years, recognising various forms of Non-Stipendiary Ministry. A man or a woman can now be ordained as an elder without becoming a salaried professional. Such people continued to get their living from their secular occupations. Alan had been headteacher of the village school for over twenty years, and would continue to be the headteacher after ordination as before. The service of ordination was for Alan the climax of five years of selection and training; a ponderous process, more designed to produce the professional élite than to equip the eldership of the local church. But then old, established thought-patterns only change slowly. Everyone needs time to adapt to new ideas and practices.

At the first meeting of the Church Council of St Nicholas' after Alan's ordination, new anxieties came to the surface. Although we had all known about Alan's ordination for years it was only after the event that the implications began to dawn on people.

'Who is our rector now?' someone asked me, 'Is it you or Alan?'

'What happens if you and Alan disagree?'

'Who do we turn to if we need help?'

Age-old patterns of life in country villages were beginning to dissolve. Easier to adapt to the idea of one vicar with several churches than to adapt to the idea of several vicars in one church.

'But who was the rector or vicar of Ephesus?' I replied. 'When Paul said farewell to the elders of Ephesus, he said, "Keep watch over yourselves and all the flock of which the Holy Spirit has made you overseers. Be shepherds of the church of God which he bought with his own blood" (Acts 20:28-29). They functioned as some sort of a team, watching over both themselves and their life together as a group, and over the rest of the flock.'

How that worked out in practice none of us knew. How to make it work in practice today, none of us knew. I guessed we should be years learning all over again about how to share leadership, ministry and oversight in the church. From my own point of view, this was the first time in twenty-five years that I had had a ministerial colleague. I was going to have to make changes to the way I went about my own work. Many things would now need to be discussed with others which previously I would have decided on my own. On the other hand there would now be two of us, and with Stephen our Reader, three of us, to share the load, to take counsel together and to do the work. As we grew together as a team I was to sense a new solidity in the work which God had done among us. No longer did I feel, as I had done for so long, that everything depended on me.

I did not know the answer to the questions about what would happen if we disagreed. Legally I hold a position in our churches as rector which is still unique, but I would not want to insist upon that except as a last resort. If Alan and Stephen and I were to find ourselves in serious disagreement I believe we would have to refer the matter to our bishop, our overseer, for guidance or resolution. Scripture gives us no examples of a divided eldership. Too much, then, should not be made of this possibility, and certainly our plans and structure should not be governed by the possibility that it could occur. We are not in the business in the kingdom of God of planning for the worst.

As we increased the number of ministers of the Word and sacraments in our two churches, and as we synchronised the main morning services at St Nicholas' and St George's, so we discovered further implications in these changes. Beforehand, the people in both churches had all related to me alone as their pastor. I had seen all those who came to church week by week, and conversed with them all, if only superficially. Now I was absent at their worship as often as I was present. Other people were presiding at the services and preaching to them. How did we keep watch over the flock corporately?

Paradoxically, it became clear that this required even more delegation. The importance of the house fellowship groups became even more pronounced, and the role of the house fellowship leaders even more crucial. This was the place where the primary watching over would have to be done. There is an interesting ratio in the very earliest days of the church: in the period between the resurrection of Jesus and the day of Pentecost the church consisted of twelve apostles and 120 believers (Acts 1:15). This suggests that there is a primary level of nurture which requires a ratio of about one leader to every ten believers. That happens to be about the size of the average house fellowship.

If more is being asked of people then more should be given. So we developed a course of lay leadership training to follow on from Alpha. It was designed to equip people like house fellowship leaders and those who were in charge of other programmes in the church, both theologically and practically. We tackled together such themes as justification and sanctification, doctrinal issues such as baptism and other religions, pastoral problems to do with money and sexuality and suffering, and practical skills like handling conflict and the dynamics of a group. We encouraged people to seek God to identify their gifts and ministries, not just within the church but in their roles and jobs in the wider world.

Developing and pastoring a church in which everyone is encouraged to discover and exercise their own ministry is a delicate operation. The right balance has to be found between giving people enough scope and giving them enough support. If people are really to learn and mature in their own giftings they need to be given enough room to develop their own ideas and programmes as they feel led by God. This means giving people enough room to make mistakes, and being ready to help them clear up the mess afterwards. To watch over people so closely that they never make mistakes means not trusting them at all. No one ever grew or flourished in that situation.

On the other hand, people need enough support and encouragement. To push a beginner out in a boat on their own and wave them off into the sunset is a recipe for disaster. While too much supervision cramps and suffocates people, not enough leaves them feeling unsupported and unappreciated. Developing new ministries in the church and helping people to realise their full potential as members of the Body of Christ means providing suitable training, continuing to watch over and care for them and for what they are doing, at the same time recognising that they too have a direct line to God and a direct responsibility to him.

Keeping the rein too tight makes a horse restive and impatient; keeping it too lose allows a horse to become disobedient and unresponsive. If the leadership exercises too much control, people become frustrated and discouraged. If the leadership does not maintain enough contact, groups within the church become independent and at variance with the rest of the body.

It can be done. There are enough models of large and growing churches, with a powerful and co-operative team of leaders, and a variety of programmes and ministries functioning harmoniously together, for us to believe that such a pattern of ministry is not only the will of God, but is also feasible.

TWENTY-THREE

—

YOU HAVE NEVER BEEN
THIS WAY BEFORE

The level of activity in our two churches was increasing. The congregations were growing, if slowly. We often seemed to take two steps forward and one step back. We would add to our number some new converts, or some new arrivals from elsewhere, only to see other people lapse or move away. It would have been wonderful if all our new Christians went on to become strong, mature members of the church. But Jesus himself warned us that it would not be so. Some of the seed falls on stony ground, where the plants spring up and start looking good, but then wither away when trials come. Other seed falls amongst thorns, which grow up with it and choke the word of God amidst the cares and riches and pleasures of life. But some seed does fall on good soil and produces abundant fruit. In spite of the disappointments there is a real harvest.

A church full of Christians with a living relationship to God is a lot more work than a churchyard full of dry bones. On the negative side each new Christian added to the church is a new problem. We are all wounded soldiers, all unhealed and unwhole people. New Christians bring with them hearts and lives which are damaged and disordered. Conversion is the beginning of God's work in them, not the end. On the positive side God will be speaking to them. The leader of a renewed church will have people coming to him saying, 'Can we form a banner group? I believe God wants us to make banners for the church.' Or, 'I feel called to work with the youth. God has given me a burden for the young people.'

I do not believe that God speaks only to me, or that all the initiative has to come from the top down. I have to help people discern what is of God and what is not; help them to discern what is for now and what is for the future; then help them to do what God is calling them to do. As far as the church goes, I have to try to hold the whole thing together: to put together the people who want to make banners and encourage them to work together; to put together the people who are called to work with youth and devise a unified programme for the church. In fact I believe that it is much more my job to discern and respond to what God is doing wherever he is at work, than to devise my own programmes for the church to follow. It is less hard work to do what God is already doing. But it is still hard work, and the work-load was increasing.

I was running out of hours and days in the week; in particular I was running out of evenings. I was exhorted to delegate more and more, which I did. But still someone has to oversee what has been delegated, someone has to support those to whom it has been delegated, and someone has to pick up the pieces when other people drop them. It is not true that delegation lessens the work-load. Delegation allows more work to be done. But in the end that increases the work-load for everyone.

Church-growth analysts all recognise that at some

point a church can only continue to grow if it takes on more paid staff. Paying people means two things: firstly more time, secondly more commitment. Volunteers can usually give only a limited number of hours of their time. They have other commitments and other jobs, which may often have to take priority over their voluntary work, even church work. The church has first claim on the time of paid staff members, at least for an agreed number of hours per week. There are exceptions to this, but as a generalisation it is true: at a certain point of growth an organisation has to employ more paid staff.

At one level, everyone in our two churches took paid staff for granted. They assumed without question that they would have a full-time, paid, rector. In recent years they had had to become accustomed to sharing this rector with another parish, but no one questioned the rightness or necessity of my existence.

In recent years Anglicans had been coming to terms with another idea: that if you wanted a rector or a vicar you would have to pay for him yourselves. From time immemorial the rector's pay has been a complete mystery to most church-goers. It was as if money floated down from heaven and appeared, like Father Christmas, out of the rectory chimney. It did not happen like that for anybody else, but it seemed to happen for the clergy. Then came the Quota. The diocese began to demand money from the parishes to pay the stipends of the clergy. By some extraordinary logic the number of stipendiary clergyman then went steadily down, while at the same time the diocesan quota went steadily up. Some parishes paid, others did not. So the cycle repeated itself, over and over again. The Church of England now seems to be locked in to an inexorable spiral of decline.

St Nicholas' and St George's paid their Quota. The

Quota went up; we continued to pay. As the congregations went up, and as the people were set free by God to give, so the offerings went up. We were not embarrassed by the increasing financial demands made upon us. But now we faced a new challenge. We needed to employ more staff of our own.

We certainly could not expect more staff from the diocese. The diocese was reducing its pay-roll, not increasing it. We had to support any new staff ourselves. But why not? Other churches did it: they paid their own administrators, or youth workers, or assistant pastors. Most of these churches were town or city churches, but what was the difference? Nevertheless it was a very foreign idea to our country villages. People found it difficult to understand that we either could or should do such a thing. But I was quite clear that without it we had hit a ceiling beyond which the churches and the work could not grow.

God provided a way for us to get used to the idea slowly. Stephen, our Reader, had been working for several years as an administrator for a charitable trust. He was an excellent organiser but also felt he had a calling from God to be a pastor and a teacher. His training as a Reader had been a step in the direction of responding to that calling. But after he joined us, we sponsored him as a candidate for the local Non-Stipendiary Ministry. He was accepted by the Church of England and started a further course of part-time training. Stephen was already responsible for running our Alpha courses. He was preaching and leading worship on a regular basis. He was involved with other areas of work particularly at St George's. For a long time we had prayed that God would raise up a leader resident in that village. Stephen's employment with his charitable trust allowed him a measure of flexibility. So we began to pay him out of our church funds to work for us for a few hours each week. As time went on we were able to increase these hours until, over a couple of years, Stephen became a full-time member of the staff. Part of his work and part of his salary came from *Living Water*, the other part from the two churches themselves.

It was not an easy transition to make. Just as people had to redefine their relationship to Alan when he was ordained, so people had to redefine their understanding of the role of Stephen when he began to be paid. There was some resentment and jealousy. In many ways it is easier to come in from outside as a total stranger and take up such a role, than to be raised up out of the body of the church. There was understandable confusion over Stephen's position. There are such things as stipendiary Readers in the Church of England but they are as rare as hen's teeth. Most people think of the office as a spare-time one. Stephen had now been accepted as a candidate for Non-Stipendiary Ministry. What were we doing paying him a stipend? I had to explain that non-stipendiary was Stephen's status from a diocesan point of view: the diocese was not accepting a responsibility to pay him on his ordination. If the parishes wanted to do so, that was our business.

As with so many other things these days we found ourselves in uncharted seas. How much should we pay Stephen? With what or with whom should we compare him in fixing a level of remuneration? What arrangements ought we to make about a pension for him? Should we tell the bishop what we were doing? And what would he say? Like the Israelites entering Canaan under the leadership of Joshua, we 'had never been this way before' (Josh 3:4).

Stephen's employment however enabled our activities both inside the parishes and outside to go on growing. In no time Stephen, or a Stephen-shaped person, had become indispensable. The level of activity in our two churches, and in giving away what we had received to the wider church, simply could not be sustained without him.

—

TWENTY-FOUR

TO SING JOYFUL SONGS

The music group at St Nicholas' had fallen apart when the leader resigned. For different reasons the arrangements at St George's were in similar disarray. For several years Linda had played both the organ and guitar at St George's (not at the same time of course). Her husband James had offered himself and been accepted as a candidate for ordination. So, with a mixture of joy and sadness we had said good-bye to James and Linda and their three children.

Musicians of any sort are difficult to find in country parishes. If you are passed on a Sunday morning in a country lane by a 'galloping' vicar, stand back. The next person down the road is quite likely to be a 'galloping' organist. In a rural area several churches may share one organist just as they share one vicar. When Linda went, there had been no replacement in sight at St George's. For a year John and Becky had held the fort. But then Becky had become pregnant and the burden of sustaining the music ministry at St George's on their own had become too great for them.

God was teaching me more lessons the hard way, with grazed knees and bloody bandages. The music ministry in the church is a spiritual battle area. Worship has such an important role in our relationship to God: it is the direct way into the Holy Place, into the presence and the heart of God. And music has such an important role in worship. In the psalms, praise is inextricably linked with singing:

> Come, let us sing for joy to the Lord;
> let us shout aloud to the Rock of our salvation.
> Let us come before him with thanksgiving
> and extol him with music and song (Ps 95:1-2).

When David brought the ark of the covenant up to Jerusalem, he gave top priority to setting up a music ministry (1 Chron 15:16-22).

Music in worship being as important as it is, we can expect that the devil will devise schemes to disrupt the musical arrangements and with them the activity of worship. For that reason the musicians and singers in the church need more attention and need to be more carefully pastored than other groups. I had ignored this need, particularly with John and Becky. Any reconstruction of the music ministry in either church would have to incorporate more support for all those involved in it from the pastoral team, Alan and Stephen and me.

Trying to fill the gaps, we faced the usual temptations to look outside the worshipping community for musical reinforcements. We knew of one or two musicians who were occasional worshippers, but not committed, as far as we knew, to Jesus, and certainly not to the church. We knew of someone else who played both the keyboard and guitar and who had made a Christian commitment in the past. But her personal life was in disorder and she would not be accountable for sorting it out.

King David had learned, also the hard way, that the

first requirement for those who ministered to the Lord was that they should be of the priestly tribe of Levi (1 Chron 15:12-13). His first attempt to bring up the ark to Jerusalem had ended in disaster when Uzzah, a non-Levite, had touched it. Uzzah dropped dead, and David was devastated (1 Chron 13:7-11). There is no separate tribe of priests within the people of the new covenant: all the members of the church are a royal priesthood. But non-believers are not. Those who minister to the Lord in worship must first of all be worshippers. It is a principle we cannot ignore.

Then, those who sang and played instruments before the Lord had to be dressed in fine linen (1 Chron 15:27). Fine linen is symbolical of righteous lives (Rev 19:8). So those who have a role in leading worship and singing in the church must be people who have washed and continue to wash their robes and make them white in the blood of the Lamb. They must walk in repentance and faith, and their lives must not be scandalous to the congregation.

So we continued to keep the fences at what I believed was the proper height. Just anyone would not do to be a member of the music group: their hearts had to be fixed on God above all, and their lives had to be in reasonable order. Last, but not least, they had to have some musical ability. Kenaniah was in charge of David's music group, 'because he was skilful at it' (1 Chron 15:22). The level of musical ability had to be such that the person's singing or playing was more a help than a hindrance to the congregation. This cannot be taken for granted. We have all sung with organists who have played the hymns so slowly that a song of praise has become a dirge. Too many wrong notes also trip a congregation up rather than help them along. The job of the musicians is not just to minister to

God but also to minister to the congregation, by leading them into the presence of God and assisting them to worship. A certain level of musical ability is necessary to do this.

Musical ability can increase. It is a sign of a person's calling and commitment to a music ministry that they are prepared to go on taking lessons and practising. But some people will never progress beyond a certain point. It is one of the hardest jobs in the world to tell someone that they simply are not good enough. Better not to take them on in the first place. On the other hand it is a real joy to see someone improving week by week and growing up into a real leader of worship.

What we had then at this point, was a pool of perhaps six instrumentalists and a similar number of singers drawn from the two churches, amongst whom no one was in a position to assume the full burden of responsibility for leading worship in either church. Up to now we had operated with a model of a single group in each church, under one leader, with a fixed membership, a group which was expected by everyone to perform week in and week out. Such an arrangement had become impossible. I did also notice that when David had set up the music ministry for the tabernacle in Jerusalem he had appointed not just one group of singers and players, but twenty-four (1 Chron 25:9-31). We had to think again.

Had one group in each church been such a good idea anyway? Every week the members of the music group had been on duty. They themselves had never had an opportunity, from one year's end to another, to sit in the congregation, to be ministered to, to worship God without worrying about the mechanics of worship. Such a régime had taken its toll already on those who had been subject to it. Perhaps we ought to be thinking of moving away from such a model.

Such a fixed arrangement also seemed to block the way in for other people. If we wanted to build up our musical resources we had to be open to new musicians and new singers joining in. There had for some time been people in the congregation at St Nicholas' who had all the qualifications to play or sing. But the seats in the music group had all been full. We had to find a way to discover what gifts God might be giving to other people and use them in his service. We had to look for a new régime.

Up to now we had expected the same person to organise the group, choose the worship songs, practise and train the group, and then lead the worship at the service. On second thoughts we saw that some of these functions could be separated. Julia was willing to take over the organisation of the groups in both parishes, and to draw up a rota month by month. We could provide a group for each church week by week which would include a worship leader, one or perhaps two instrumentalists, and two or three singers. It would not be the same group from week to week, but this would make it possible for people to have a break and to worship in the congregation, and this would make it possible for new people to come in and try out a calling to the music ministry.

Everyone would meet together twice a month, not just to practice and play together, but for fellowship. One of the pastoral team would join them and we could share our burdens and pray for one another before we ministered to the Lord. For events other than our regular Sunday services, events like our monthly celebration on the first Saturday, we could pick up a team which would combine the resources of both churches. Change is never easy or painless, but perhaps after all God was leading us into a better way than we had had before.

It took several months for us to see where God was leading and to put the new system in place. During those months the whole problem was a considerable anxiety to me. In theory I know that these churches are God's and not mine. In practice I find it much harder to trust all the implications of that. If God really values worship, as I believe he does, then will he not provide the resources for it? Everything is in God's hands. The difficulties and setbacks come, if not according to his will, at least with his permission. The proper reaction is to say, 'What is God teaching us now?' Too often we sink instead into anxiety or despair. Whatever size and at whatever stage of growth churches are, they will always have problems – not least in the area of music.

—

TWENTY-FIVE

YOU WILL SPREAD OUT

We quickly ran out of space. We had two narrow aisles, a small area of carpet at the front and another at the back. Apart from that, St Nicholas' was wall-to-wall pews. At the informal service on the first Saturday of the month we had, as usual, invited those who wanted prayer and ministry to step out of the pews and find some open space. Soon, so many people were lying on the carpet under the power of the Holy Spirit that we were in trouble. A large lady collapsed on top of the person behind her. The ministry team tried to unstack them and find enough floor for each of them to have a little. Another couple were staggering under the weight of a man who was also falling and looked as if he would hit his head on a radiator. One ministry team member was saying to another, 'Could you move your person's leg; your person's foot is kicking my person's head'. We could not do anything about it.

There was a certain inflexibility about the furniture of the church which affected other things as well as the ministry of the Holy Spirit. My predecessor at St Nicholas' had carried through a scheme which had reordered the old chancel. The chancel arch had been glazed, thus cutting the chancel off from the main body of the church. The choir stalls and other furniture had been removed and the whole area was now carpeted. More recently we had created a small kitchen. The chancel-room, furnished with comfortable chairs, was now ideal for small meetings and for Sunday school, but with forty people in it, it was full to capacity. From time to time we held meetings and courses for which this room was not big enough. But the main body of the church gave us no flexibility. People could sit in rows facing the front, but any sort of discussion in smaller groups in which we needed to face each other was impossible.

The bell-ringers had mounted an exhibition of campanology in connection with the rehanging of St Nicholas' six bells, but exhibits had to be laid out horizontally on boards across the tops of the pews. Vertical display boards were impossible with pews touching the walls on both sides of the church. Even a flower-festival had had to be crammed into corners because there was so little open space.

If our activities and God's were to be set free from the constraints of space we had to remove the pews. The reordering of the chancel ten years before had caused a good deal of controversy at the time. Now it was difficult to find anyone who did not think it was a brilliant idea. Probably the same thing would happen with the pews. I decided to suggest that we start in a small way. The side aisle was clearly distinct from the nave. It would be possible to remove the pews in the aisle without interfering too drastically with anything else. This area could then be carpeted and the seating replaced with comfortable chairs. This part of the church at least could then be used in a variety of ways. The chairs could be arranged in rows, or circles, or stacked away altogether. If the new flexibility proved its worth, then it would still be possible to extend the arrangement to the rest of the church at a later date.

When the church council came to consider the matter, the usual issues were raised. They were decent pews, not particularly old, not particularly elegant, but good solid oak, well made and likely to last for years to come. Was it not a shame to get rid of such good furniture in favour of chairs that probably would not last half as long? What about our responsibility as guardians of our heritage? These pews were part of our inheritance: had we the right to dispose of them?

The obsession of our age with preserving anything that is old was not one which our forefathers themselves shared. The Victorians who had made these very pews confidently believed that they were improving on what had gone before and furnished the church according to their views and requirements without a backward look. In the Middle Ages the nave of the church would have been one large open space; perhaps some benches against the walls for the old and infirm, but not a pew or a chair in sight. People would come in and stand to hear Mass, said in the sanctuary by the priest. At other times in the week, it is said, other village activities might take place in the nave, even dances. The sense of sacredness did not extend beyond the chancel arch.

At the Reformation the spaces were reversed, the holy table was moved into the nave, and the chancel became a place to keep ladders and brooms and cobwebs. The main body of the church became the sacred place; the chancel became a bogey-hole. The Victorians restored the chancels, put the altars back at the east end, installed organs and robed choirs, and filled the nave with pews.

Worship changed in the Victorian era. In most village churches up to then the singing of hymns had been accompanied by the church band, a little group of rustic musicians playing, perhaps, a violin, a cello, a clarinet or a trumpet. Many parsons disliked the band: an unruly and unmusical thorn in their flesh. Organs played in tune; they certainly made more noise, and parsons imagined that organists would be easier to control than bands. The Victorians fell in love with Anglican chant, an arcane and complicated way of singing psalms and other non-metrical canticles. Soon the Sunday services of Mattins and Evensong were being chanted from beginning to end, and a competent performance required a trained choir. The whole traumatic process of evicting the band and installing an organ and an organist is vividly described in Thomas Hardy's novel *Under the Greenwood Tree.*

As the worship became more dignified and orderly, so the congregation too had to be brought into line – literally. Pews made sure that people sat in rows and ranks, like soldiers on parade. Pews did not permit walking or running about. Pews allowed people to squeeze up if the congregation continued to grow. The present ordering and furnishing of our churches was not so old after all. Our great-grandfathers had wanted it that way, but we had as much right as them to move the furniture to suit the needs and tastes of our own generation.

Ideas of worship were changing again. Whatever the beauties of choral Mattins and Evensong the population at large had long since stopped appreciating them. In most churches these rows and rows of brown Victorian pews resembled the furrows of a field in which nothing ever seemed to come up. Our worship now needed more informality, more flexibility, more creative uses of space. We wanted to dance in church, wave banners, use drama and mime, have coffee and even meals. We wanted to be able to face each other as well as God, and, if God wanted us to do so, to fall down.

It was still hard for people to part with the pews. The church council supported the idea, as did most of the worshippers. The trouble started when the news hit the streets. People who were married in the church years before wrote to me accusing me of sacrilege. One horrified parishioner alerted the local newspaper, and to my amazement St Nicholas' pews became a national sensation. For two days my life was consumed with interviews for radio, television, and the press. Why on earth should the nation be interested in the doings round our parish pump? Eventually I realised that our pews were a symbol of something more: of an historic transition in the life of the Church.

God was indeed doing something new. Hounds with a nose for news had scented it and wanted to write about it. People in the village had not recognised it or did not want to know about it. There were undoubtedly some who were living in hope that our new ways were just a passing fad. Rectors, with their idiosyncrasies, had come and gone, leaving the village church to go on much as before. This rector would go too, one day. But the removal of the pews was something different: a final good-bye. The pews were more than furniture; they were totems. Their removal would mean that there was no going back. A furniture-removal van at the church gate would be a prophetic sign that the Church was moving on.

—

TWENTY-SIX

AND FOR YOUR CHILDREN

The Apostle Peter said, 'The promise is for you and for your children.' The promise was this: 'Repent and be baptised, every one of you, in the name of Jesus Christ for the forgiveness of your sins. And you will receive the gift of the Holy Spirit' (Acts 2:38-39).

We do seem to have very muddled ideas about children and the things of God. Apparently it was always the same. On one occasion parents were bringing their children to Jesus that he might touch them, and the texts stress that these were little children, even babies (Mk 10:13, Lk 18:15). The point about Jesus touching them was that this was the only meaningful contact he could have with them: he could not talk to them, they were too small to understand words. So he took them in his arms and put his hands on them as a sign of blessing. The disciples would have stopped it. They probably thought that such children were too young to come to Jesus: children must wait until they were grown up like them. Jesus however turned their ideas upside down. 'On the contrary,' he said, 'you must become children, like them.' Children might not be able to repent and believe the gospel, which was Jesus' invitation to the adults (Mk 1:15), but children could still come to him; and children could enter the kingdom of God (Mk 10:13-16).

Peter, it appears, learned the lesson, for on the day of Pentecost he said, 'The promise is for you and your children'. Some people deny that the word 'children' means children; they say it means descendants, generations still to come; your children when they are grown up like us. The Bible does sometimes use the word 'children' in that sense. But it is most unlikely that that is what is meant here.

Firstly, Peter had been taught by Jesus that even babies who could not repent could be received into the kingdom of God. Secondly, Peter was a Jew and was speaking to a Jewish audience. The Jews were not just permitted but commanded to make their sons children of the covenant at the age of eight days (Gen 17:11-13). So the idea that the children of Christians, even babies, could become children of the new covenant would not have seemed strange to Peter. Indeed it would have seemed strange to any Jew if his children should be excluded. Thirdly, there are indications in the New Testament that many in the generation of the apostles expected that the return of the Lord was imminent, in their own life-time (1 Cor 15:51). In which case Peter was not anticipating generations of descendants for his hearers; he meant, 'the promise is for you and your children now.'

Christians still seem to be muddled about all this. Some deny baptism to infants and children, on the grounds that they cannot repent and believe: children must wait until they are grown up like us. (Where have we heard that before?) Some dogmatically deny that children and infants can be born again: they are old enough to be born, but not old enough to be born again; they must wait until they are grown up like us. Others believe that children should be shielded from the Holy Spirit: let them wait until they are grown up like us. Yet no Christian wants to deny that children, even infants, can be saved and have everlasting life. What a muddle!

Children, even babies, can come to Jesus. Christian parents will want to bring their babies to Jesus just as the parents in the Bible did. Jesus will receive them and bless them. Coming to Jesus, they come into the Kingdom of God, for Jesus is the King. Jesus is the one who forgives sins; he is the source of everlasting life; he is the baptiser in the Holy Spirit. Just as Jewish babies were circumcised as a sign that they were children of the old covenant, so the babies of Christian parents are baptised as a sign that they are children of the new covenant. Baptism is the new circumcision (Col 2:11).

As children of the new covenant, Christian children are inheritors of all the promises of God, or of none. If they have a right to everlasting life, they also have a right to the forgiveness of sins and to the gift of the Holy Spirit. It is impossible to award to children some of the promises and not others. If small children are incapable of repentance and faith then God does not require it of them. When they do become capable of repentance and faith God does require it of them. Under the old covenant Jewish boys, at the age of twelve, including Jesus, became *bar mitzvah*: not just a child of the covenant but a child of the commandment. Up to that age a boy was not regarded as being responsible for the fulfilment of the law in his own right; he was under the authority of his parents who were responsible to God for him. At the age of twelve the boy took on the responsibility for himself. So I believe it is with Christian children. Up to about the age of twelve they are covered by their parents' repentance and faith. About that age they need to be encouraged to take on the responsibility for themselves. But children do not have to wait until they are grown up like us to enter the kingdom of God and to receive the benefits of the kingdom, forgiveness, eternal life, and the gifts of the Holy Spirit.

Children brought up in a Christian home do not have any difficulty in believing in God or believing in Jesus; likewise Christian children do not have any difficulty with the theory and practice of spiritual gifts. Speaking in tongues may alarm certain adults but children just think it is fun. Adults often have difficulty adjusting their view of the world to the miraculous. Children do not have a view of the world to adjust, and are much more open to the idea of a God who acts. Some adults are alarmed by people falling down under the power of the Spirit and lying on the carpet, children just step over them.

Sarah-Jane was eleven years old. She had suffered with an allergy to lactose since birth. This meant that if she ate or drank any milk product, milk, cream, butter, or cheese, she was sick and came out in an itching rash. For the last four years she had also suffered with asthma, and, like so many children today, had to take an inhaler to school with her every day.

One day she was at a Christian meeting where the children were being encouraged to pray for each other, especially for those with asthma. Sarah-Jane put her hand up for prayer, and three of her friends, Mary, Lisa and Leah, all around the same age, laid hands on her and prayed for the Holy Spirit to come and heal her of asthma. Sarah-Jane fell down under the power of the Spirit, and felt herself being healed, not just of asthma but of her lactose allergy as well. It was as if someone were telling her to go out and drink some milk.

When she stood up again she went back and told

Brenda, her mother, that she had been healed, and wanted a glass of milk. Her mother, of course, was very doubtful about the wisdom of this, but nevertheless, over the next few days, allowed Sarah-Jane to try increasing amounts of milk, butter, cheese and cream. No adverse reactions; Sarah-Jane's stomach accepted the lactose and digested it in all its forms. One week later she was due for a routine appointment with the consultant paediatrician. The paediatrician was very reluctant to admit to miracles, but had to confess that Sarah-Jane did seem to have suddenly grown out of her allergy. One year later Sarah-Jane was discharged to eat as many cream cakes as she liked.

Her healing from asthma was no less immediate and dramatic. As soon as she had returned home Sarah-Jane had blown into her peak-flow machine. Her exhalation at once registered twice what she had been able to achieve over the previous four years. Since then she has had no asthma attacks and has simply stopped taking her inhaler to school.

Eight-year-old Simon went to a class where the children were being taught about how God speaks in dreams and visions. Going to bed that night, he was lying awake with his eyes open when he began to see words in front of him. The words seemed to be jumbled up as in a puzzle, and he had to sort them out so as to make a sentence. Simon enjoyed puzzles like that and he soon saw the meaning: 'Simon, your sins are forgiven'. Contentedly he turned over and went to sleep. It was not until he was settling down to bed the following evening that he remembered his vision of the previous night. He called his mother. His mother thought that there must be something wrong, but to her surprise her eight-year-old announced, 'I had a vision last night. I have not had one of those before'.

Twins Steven and Andrew were only six when they went with their family to a Christian conference. Early in the week their older brother and sister, David and Kathryn, had been filled with the Holy Spirit, but the Holy Spirit had not yet been invited to visit the meeting of five and six-year-olds. The twins were rather disappointed to hear that they had missed out on something, and asked their father why they could not have the Holy Spirit too. Their parents, Richard and Jo, talked to them about the Holy Spirit, and when they were satisfied that their six-year-olds understood all that six-year-olds can understand about the Holy Spirit, they prayed that Jesus would send his Spirit to Steven and Andrew too.

Andrew immediately fell on the floor laughing and began to roll around helplessly. Steven on the other hand remained perfectly still and upright. Why was not the same thing happening to him? (Have not we all asked that question?) Richard tried to explain, as usual, that the Holy Spirit touched people in different ways, but to a six-year-old it still did not seem fair. So Richard offered to pray for Steven again.

'Do you feel anything at all?' he enquired.

'I feel a sort of little pain in my tummy,' Steven replied. 'Not a hurt, but a sort of pain.'

Richard was reminded of a song the children sang:

It's a joy from deep inside
Only Jesus can provide.
I'm gonna let the joy of Jesus overflow.
> (Captain Alan Price)

As he sang these words Richard made a rolling motion with his fingers, coming up from Steven's tummy. When he reached Steven's throat, the laughter burst out, and Steven was on the floor, too, rolling round in the same state of helpless merriment as Andrew. The promise is indeed for you and your children.

TWENTY-SEVEN

NO ONE ELSE DARED JOIN THEM

A considerable gap had opened up between the church and the village in both parishes. Over a number of years the service had been changing. First the services had been modernised, the modern service book instead of the old Prayer Book, modern songs as well as ancient hymns. The population at large had long since voted with their feet on the old services, so it was not that something they treasured had been taken away from them. Nevertheless the words we said and the songs we sang were now no longer familiar to those who joined us occasionally.

A larger gap had opened up as the services became more overtly charismatic. Our way of worshipping in song for fifteen or twenty minutes, the public use of the gifts of the Spirit, and the ministry of healing made it increasingly difficult for strangers to the church to know what was going on. Then came the public manifestations of the Holy Spirit in the middle of the main Sunday services. The stories and the rumours, no doubt suitably embellished, about what was now going on in the churches made the gap between the congregation and the community in both villages a yawning chasm.

Underlying the overt signs of change, the spirituality of the worshipping congregations had been changing too. Our Christians no longer shared the comfortable, undemanding nostrums of folk-religion: 'You don't have to go to church to be a Christian', 'I'm as good as those who go to church', 'We're all going to the same place in the end'. Our Christians had found a personal relationship with Jesus; they had been filled with the life-giving Spirit of God. Above all, it was they who had changed. All the changes in the services were the result of changes in the people. The real chasm was between the people who came to church and the people who did not.

This went against much of the traditional understanding of the relationship between the parish church and the community with which I had been brought up. The Church of England by its history and position in the land is supposed to be inclusive rather than exclusive. In times past I had spoken quite eloquently myself about the church as a focus for the spiritual aspirations of all the people of the parish, however vague those aspirations might be; of the church as the Godward face of the community, representing the parish, however vicariously, before God. The trouble was, God seemed to have other ideas about the relationship of church and community.

I could not repent of the way we had come. I could not repent of the changes in the people: they certainly did not repent of them themselves. I could not repent of any of the changes in our worship. Either we were reaching out to God with all our hearts and minds and strength or we were not. If we were, this was where our aspirations had led us. And there it was in the Scriptures: the relationship between Jesus and his contemporaries, and the relationship between the apostolic church and its world, was not the comfortable, easy contact of the rural, Anglican idyll.

Jesus said, 'I did not come to bring peace, but a sword' (Matt 10:34). Over and over again people were divided by him (Jn 7:43, 9:16, 10:19). And this was no quiet, tolerant, difference of opinion; this was violent, murderous hate. Should it be any different today? Should we not expect there to be a chasm between the believers and the unbelievers? Indeed can it be right if there is not? They said that Jesus was mad (Mk 3:21) and possessed by Beelzebub (Mk 3:22); something is wrong when all men speak well of us (Lk 6:26).

I was comforted to discover that the same gap had existed between the early church and the population of Jerusalem. 'All the believers used to meet together in Solomon's Colonnade. No one else dared join them...Nevertheless, more and more men and women believed in the Lord and were added to their number' (Acts 5:12-14). There was a fear of going near these Christians and their gatherings (Acts 2:43), which nevertheless did not hinder the flow of conversions. People did not drift casually in and out of the church, as if it were merely an alternative form of entertainment, as they tend to do today. There was a serious gulf to be crossed, and it required a serious decision to cross it. That was the position we now found ourselves in at St George's and St Nicholas'.

Our next realisation was that it was our job to build bridges back across that gulf, bridges over which people could come into the kingdom of God. The bridges have always had to be built from the Godward side. The ultimate gap between God himself and a sinful world had to be bridged from God's side: God had to send his own Son to be the bridge in his human flesh. The mission of the church has always been to go out and build new bridges with the unbelieving world.

St George's decided to hold a parish audit. Church members visited every house in the village with a questionnaire. There were questions to elicit information about social needs: how many under-fives would be coming in to the village school in the next few years? The village school was already bursting at the seams and we needed to know how many more children would need accommodation in the future. There were questions about the provision for the social needs of other age groups in the village, and what might be lacking. Finally there were questions about the church: had people ever gone to church, if so when did they stop and why? Would they like to be visited? The whole exercise was devised as valid in itself, but also as a way of making personal contact with everyone in the parish and hearing what they had to say about the village and the church.

St Nicholas' took a somewhat different approach. Here, we had some years before conducted a house-to-house visitation. We had not asked questions, merely offered each household an evangelistic booklet and a tract we had produced ourselves in which four well-known people in the village told of how they had found Jesus. There was an opportunity to talk with the householders, but few of them responded in any positive way. 'Cold-calling', as the salesmen describe it, is not a very profitable form of contact. Whether it is double-glazing or Christianity, few people welcome the intrusion. Cold-calling does produce occasional results, or not even the salesmen would persevere with it, but we had learnt the hard way that personal relationships need to be built up before most people will receive the gospel from us.

The bridges we had to build were bridges of acquaintance, trust and service. Once we got the task into focus, we saw that God had already provided us with plenty of opportunities. Everyone had next-door neighbours. People who went to work had colleagues and mates. The mothers met each other in the playground. The village streets and the shop were still places where people stopped to chat. We already had entries into most of the village organisations: the WI, the Village Hall Management Committee, and the old folks club. Brian was the secretary of the village car-scheme which provided lifts for people to the doctor. Alan ran the village youth club. The church had three governors in the school, and other Christian parents were involved in the Parent-Teacher Association.

It was a question of getting involved in the village activities and making the most of the opportunities we already had. Church life so easily acts as a sponge, soaking up all the time and energy Christians have. As the church grows so the meetings and programmes multiply until people can be at a church function every night of the week. We had to resist this temptation and consciously go out into the community around us, and build bridges.

There had to be no ulterior motives. People are quick to detect confidence tricks. The friendships and the service had to be genuine, an end in themselves, not merely a cover for evangelism. Only when we had proved ourselves as friends and neighbours, as colleagues and helpers, would people trust us with their questions and problems. But if we proved ourselves as friends the opportunities would come. The personal relationships were not bridges over which we could rush out to proclaim the Good News; they were the bridges over which people outside could cross over into the kingdom of God when the time was ripe.

Fiona lived near to Lorraine, and sitting out-of-doors during the summer while their children played, they became friends. When Fiona got a part-time job it was natural to ask Lorraine to mind her children while she worked. This brought the two young mothers into more regular contact with one another, and once or twice their conversation touched on the fact that Fiona and her family came to church. One day it seemed right to invite Lorraine and her toddler to come to the Edward Bear service. This was a short, simple service for mothers and toddlers held in St George's on a weekday afternoon before the older children came out of school. Lorraine and Bethany came, and enjoyed it.

Over the next few weeks Lorraine and her husband Ivan began to talk to Fiona and her husband Daryl more seriously about God. Ivan began to read the Bible and soon wanted to talk about God more than anything else. The next time we had a service on the first Saturday Lorraine was there with Daryl and Fiona. As we invited the Holy Spirit to come Fiona began to shake, and soon she and several others were slain in the Spirit in the aisle. Daryl inquired whether Lorraine would like someone to pray for her. 'I don't want anyone to throw me on the floor,' she replied. But she did accept prayer and God did put her on the floor. God changed Lorraine that night, and when she went home Ivan saw the difference, in her and in their relationship. From then on Ivan wanted it too.

Ivan, Lorraine and family went to tea with Daryl and Fiona and announced that they wanted to start coming to church. So the next Sunday a new family appeared at St George's. For some reason Ivan kept wanting to cry, but stopped himself until the end. Then he too gave way and allowed the tears to flow as God filled him up with

Himself. Fiona had built a bridge, and Ivan and Lorraine, Aaron and Bethany had stepped across it into the kingdom of God.

—

TWENTY-EIGHT

TURN THE HEARTS OF THE FATHERS TO THE CHILDREN

Moving house is a stressful and disorientating experience. Jan had just moved into one of our villages and was at the stage of wondering what she was doing here. Jan had become a Christian ten years before, but had then undergone some searing, personal experiences and fallen away from the Lord. She had become an expert in reading tarot cards and developed a dual personality: one half of her laid out the cards while the other half told her it was wrong.

Now she was married to Chris and with her own children, David, Hayley and Michael, and a nephew Daniel she had come to live in the country. Their cottage was right opposite St George's church, and Jan began to go in during the day when the church was empty in search of the God she had known and lost. On the wall of St George's was a vast oil-painting of the risen Jesus appearing to the disciples in the upper room. One day Jan was looking at this picture and she said, 'Jesus, I don't know how to come back to you.'

Later she took her Bible out onto the village playing-field to read it. She asked God to show her what he wanted her to do in this strange village. The wind flicked over the pages and she read, 'I have heard your prayer' (2 Chron 7:12). On the other side of the playing-field was a play-area for the smaller children with swings and a slide and a climbing frame. Messing about on this equipment were a group of teenagers. Jan went over to them and started to talk to them. They were bored and aggressive, resentful of a world which seemed to offer them nothing but rejection and condemnation.

'I'll play a game with you if you like,' Jan offered.

'Go on then. What are we going to play?' they asked.

'See this book,' said Jan indicating her Bible, 'there is a secret message in it. You've got to capture the book and discover the message.'

The game Jan devised kept the boys occupied for the rest of the afternoon. The secret message at the end of it was John 3:16: 'For God so loved the world that he gave his one and only Son, that whoever believes in him shall not perish but have everlasting life'. When the time came to go home the boys said, 'Please can we play that game again?'.

Over the next few weeks Jan made friends with these boys and they started to visit her house. They came to lounge about in her sitting room, to drink her coffee, to talk to Jan about their homes, their school, their parents. They also ruined her garden, broke her windows and set fire to her caravan. The church also suffered broken windows and graffiti on the walls. Several of these boys were in trouble with the police, and were to go on probation for arson and theft. For one of them at least the next step was Borstal. Jan's neighbours were not best pleased with the company she was keeping. 'Some people you can never help,' she was told.

Nevertheless Jan persevered. It was not easy for her

own family. Her own children had to be considered, and not exposed to danger. Chris, her husband, found it difficult to have his own place invaded by these unruly strangers. Still Jan persevered. The boys started to respect her. She made them go round and apologise to the neighbours. She helped them scrub the graffiti off the church walls. God gave Jan a love for these boys which they began to sense and appreciate. All of them had been hurt and damaged by broken homes or ill-treatment. None of them had known before the sort of unconditional love which Jan was giving them.

As well as themselves and their problems Jan talked to them about Jesus. She told them he had died for their sins. They began to ask questions and to read the Bible together. After two years of patient perseverance Jan announced to me one day that three of the boys had become Christians and wanted to be baptised. They came to church the following Sunday and after the service said a prayer of commitment together at the altar rail. Soon after, a fourth, then a fifth, then a sixth, joined the growing band. They continued to meet at Jan's house and one evening a week now became a time of more explicitly Christian fellowship. Each Sunday there was this row of boys in church, still awkward with worship and our unfamiliar ways, but there for all to see.

The congregation of St George's, to their eternal credit, welcomed them and tried to make them feel at home. Not long ago they had been public enemy number one. Now they were church-goers. There were those in the village who were not as pleased at this as they might have been. 'It won't last. They are just conning you,' we were told. Others who never darkened the church door themselves did not think it was right that bad boys like that should come to church; the church was for decent people. Praise God that is not so: the church is for sinners who want to find peace with God and a new life.

The boys did not become saints overnight, but they did begin to change. I instructed them as best I could about the meaning of baptism and we hired the swimming-pool at the nearby Country House Hotel. One by one they stepped down into the water to bury the old self with Christ in baptism and rise again to a new life in fellowship with him.

'Andrew...David...Lee...Mark...Daniel...Martin, I baptise you in the name of the Father and of the Son and of the Holy Spirit.' Some of their parents were there to witness this solemn event. One of them admitted, 'This is the first school holiday when we have not had the police on the doorstep.' That was progress. I have not yet heard that being baptised enhances the street credibility of teenage boys; church-going is not good for the macho image. Whatever the problems still to be faced, I was sure that these boys were real.

Jesus said, 'Make disciples...baptise them...teach them.' Jan had made these boys disciples. I had baptised them. But we both knew that we did not have the gifts and experience to teach them. I had seen a similar move of God in St Nicholas' amongst a group of teenage girls several years before, but in the end it had all disappeared, like water into the sand. We had not had the resources or the expertise to teach them. I was anxious that we should not make the same mistake again.

Not many adults can relate well to teenagers. Jan's gift was a very special one. Of the adults who can relate to teenagers, very few have the training and knowledge to nurture them in the Christian faith. I tried all the avenues I could think of in our own locality, and drew a blank. Then I heard that one of our friends in Youth for Christ who had helped to run the youth event at *Living Water* was available on a part-time basis. Neville was a trained Christian youth-worker with several years' experience of working with young offenders in the county jail. It seemed as if he was tailor-made for our situation. Neville came out and met Jan and the boys. They all seemed to hit it off together.

But Neville had to live. He needed part of a salary as well as part-time work. We called the church councils together and told them the needs and the opportunities we now had. Again to their eternal credit, both churches did not hesitate; 'We will find the money,' they said. Even this rural area was facing a mounting problem of teenage vandalism and crime, drug-dealing and witchcraft. The police were aware of it; the traders in the High Street were aware of it; Town and Parish Councillors were aware of it. Parents were frightened for their children's future and the school struggled to deal with delinquent pupils. Now God seemed to have opened a door into this teenage world, and we were determined not to let the opportunity slip away. The fact that we had already faced so many of the issues over the employment of Stephen smoothed the path for the employment of Neville. It was time to stop wringing our hands over the problem of youth and put our hands in our pockets instead. We did.

This generation of young people is a broken and a hurting generation. Many have experienced broken homes and the absence of a mother or father; some have experienced physical and sexual abuse. They are spiritually lost, with no meaning or purpose to their lives, no love or sense of value to hold on to. This may not excuse anti-social behaviour, but it goes a long way to explaining it. What they need is not punishment and yet more rejection, but some living evidence that someone actually loves them and values them: Jan gave them that. Above all else they need God.

—

TWENTY-NINE

SO THEY BROUGHT UP THE ARK

It was now six months since we had first attempted to introduce the ministry of the Holy Spirit to the Sunday morning services. Then we had had to stop, to clear up the mess. But now it was time to try again.

When David first proposed to bring the ark of God back to Jerusalem it seemed a good plan to him and to all the people. But the project ended in disaster, with the death of Uzzah. At that point David called the whole project off, leaving the ark at the house of Obed-Edom (1 Chron 13:1-14). However, it was not the idea that was wrong, only the way of carrying it out. God was not displeased at the ark being brought up to Jerusalem. But David should have thought more carefully and enquired of God how it was to be done. So three months later, after time for reflection, David tried again. The second time, all went well. David had seen his mistakes and put them right. The Levites carried the ark in the proper manner: they used poles instead of the ox-cart, and non-Levites kept out of reach. So the ark of God came up to Jerusalem with singing and dancing and rejoicing (1 Chron 15: 28-29).

I had made the same mistake as David – at least I was in good company! The idea was right, but I had not taken enough care about how to do it. We had all had time for reflection, to learn the lessons of the past. Now it was time to try again.

The first requirement was to prepare the congregations more thoroughly for what was to happen. One way and another we had now spent the last few months explaining the ministry of the Spirit, so the job was at least partially done. It was indeed something of a cleft stick. What caused the fear and disturbance among the people were the manifestations of the Holy Spirit. So something needed to be said about these to allay the fears and reassure people about what might happen. Yet drawing attention to the manifestations only too easily draws our attention away from what really matters, the fruit in people's lives. Describing manifestations before they occur, in case they occur, is to invite charges of manipulation. Preparing people for manifestations of the Holy Spirit also runs the risk of creating disappointment and even guilt in those for whom they do not occur. It is so difficult to get it right.

However, it is impossible to reassure people too often that God is in control and that God knows what he is doing. Those are the two premises on which we embark on this ministry and they need to be stated over and over again. Very often we ourselves do not know what God is doing, but we trust that he does. Sometimes we may feel inclined to question the wisdom of what God is doing, but we have to trust that he knows best. These are faith-building exercises in themselves, and will be useful in other circumstances, as well as when faced with manifestations of the Holy Spirit.

We also had to make provision for people who would

come in, as it were, half-way through the film. We might explain the ministry of the Holy Spirit so well and so thoroughly that every member of the existing congregations was entirely at ease about it. We might do it so often that people became confident 'swimmers' in the river of God. Then someone new would come in, a visitor, an occasional worshipper, a searcher, someone facing real trouble or grief. What would they do? How could we help them to understand and receive the blessing of the Holy Spirit? Of course they might be touched and caught up into what God was doing without any need of human help or mediation. On the other hand they might be frightened and bewildered as others had been. Some might say that we just had to trust God to handle that problem, but we felt we had a responsibility ourselves to make some provision for such people. This was not a once-for-all job, but something we had to build in to the structure of the church.

We gave the job to the welcomers. Each church had a team of welcomers, members of the congregation who stood near the door on Sundays, shook hands and welcomed all who came to worship. It had long made for a sense of warmth and friendliness even towards the regular worshippers. But the special job of the welcomers was to watch out for strangers or irregular church-goers. Without gushing all over them, the welcomers were to greet people who might feel shy or out of place in church, help them to find a comfortable place to sit and make sure they had been given the appropriate books or song-sheets.

We now provided the welcomers with a short leaflet explaining the way we worshipped and what to expect during the service. The leaflet was to be given to strangers and visitors with the suggestion that they might read it in a couple of minutes before the service began. Then, after the service, the welcomers needed to be on duty again near the door to say good-bye. Without being nosey they needed to be sensitive to anyone who might be confused or upset by what had happened to them or to other people in church. An offer of a chat over a cup of coffee or a visit during the week might provide an opportunity for further conversation or reassurance. We could not guarantee that no one would go home shaking their head, but we could make sure that no one was simply left to sink or swim.

We also had to establish 'safe areas'. For a long time we had had a ministry team whose job it was to lay hands on and pray for people according to their individual needs. In a more general time of ministry in the Spirit, this team had also been accustomed to move amongst the congregation, and where they saw manifestations of the Holy Spirit, to bless what God was doing. But this too could seem threatening to people who did not know or did not like what was happening. So we had to designate the pews as out of bounds to the ministry team. Anyone who wanted to receive prayer or blessing personally had to be instructed to move out of the pews into open space, into the aisles, or to the front or the side of the church. This very act of moving would be a sign, not only to the ministry team but to God himself, that this person was hungry or thirsty, and this would increase the blessing that they would receive. But people needed to have a place where they could sit or stand or watch until such time as they were ready to step out of their own accord. So we designated the pews as 'safe areas'. In the pews God might still get them, but at least they were safe from the ministry team.

Then there was the question of the children. Our

Sunday congregations had a good proportion of children, from babes in arms to teenagers. During the ministry of the Word, the children withdrew; the toddlers to a play area or crèche, the children to Sunday school and the teenagers to a class of their own. At what point were families to be reunited in relation to the ministry of the Holy Spirit? It was not that we were afraid to expose children to the Holy Spirit. One of the reassurances that the manifestations of the Spirit are not evil is that in general neither children nor animals are disturbed by them. But it is quite difficult for a mother to concentrate on Jesus and receive a blessing from him when her toddler is tugging at her skirt and saying, 'Can we go home now? I want a drink and a biscuit.' We had to be prepared to go on looking after the children in various ways during the ministry of the Spirit. We had to provide the drink and the biscuit ourselves, while mother and father met with Jesus.

Finally we had recognised that we could not combine the ministry of the Spirit with the ministry of the sacrament. On alternate Sundays our main morning service in either church was a service of Holy Communion. We had tried to combine this with the ministry of the Spirit but it simply did not work. Whichever we did first, the second was an anti-climax. I had never seen a model for such a combination and our own experiments had not been a success.

The problem is probably that the two ministries, the ministry of the sacrament and the ministry of the Spirit are in fact much closer to one another than appears at first sight. Both are ways in which we draw near to and meet with Jesus. In the sacrament of Holy Communion we meet with Jesus over the bread and wine. In some mysterious way, because his word has made it so, as we eat this bread and drink this cup we eat the flesh and drink the blood of the Lord (Jn 6:53-56, Matt 26:26-28). It is interesting that Wesley sometimes records the same sort of manifestations at the sacrament as at his preaching.

> Poor Richard Jeffs, who, in spite of his former conviction, was now determined to renounce us, and join the Quakers, ventured, however, once more to the Lord's Table. He had no sooner received than he dropped down, and cried with a loud voice, 'I have sinned; I have sinned against God.' At that instant many were pierced to the heart. I could hardly speak for some time. Several mourners were filled with strong consolation; and all said, 'Surely God is in this place!' (Journal 4th November 1744).

At what else do we aim in the ministry of the Holy Spirit than the same meeting with Jesus? We ask the Holy Spirit to come in order that he may take the things of Jesus and make them known to us (Jn 16:14-15). It is always the work of the Holy Spirit to glorify the Son, just as it is the work of the Son to glorify the Father. Thus, the ministry of the sacrament and the ministry of the Spirit are both to lead us to Jesus. It is therefore a mistake to repeat one after the other on the same occasion. So we reintroduced the ministry of the Spirit at the service of the Word.

—

THIRTY

IN WRATH REMEMBER MERCY

I was doing more 'carpet-time' myself. Two members of the church had been praying for me at the end of a meeting. One prayed that I might have clarity of vision. As the Holy Spirit touched me I felt that backwards pressure that I had felt before, and that many seem to feel. I could probably have resisted it if I had wanted to; I could have stepped back to prevent myself from falling or recovered my balance and remained standing. But I had encouraged people on many occasions to go along with what God was doing: 'If God is making you cry, then cry; if God is causing you to laugh, then laugh; if God is pushing you over, then go.' So I went.

Once laid out on the carpet I was sufficiently conscious of my surroundings to think what a peculiar business this was. Here were about forty adults of various ages, and about half of us were lying in various attitudes on the floor. I could not think of anywhere else where people behaved in such a strange way. What this could have to do with God was difficult to see. Yet I was also conscious of his presence as I lay on the carpet, and I turned my attention to him.

Words of prayer came into my mind, very clearly

formed, Scriptural words. But the words were so inappropriate to the business of the meeting just finished, and so far from any thoughts of mine, that I guessed they were from God: 'Enter not into judgement with thy servant O Lord: for in thy sight shall no man living be justified' (Ps 143:2 Book of Common Prayer Translation). I did not know whether I was to pray this for myself or for someone else, but since it explicitly applies to everyone I started to pray it for myself. This went on for some time; a strong spirit of prayer and repentance was upon me. After a while other words began to come to me. The words were not clear, only the sense. I knew these were also from Scripture though I could not place them: something about 'renew…in our time'. As I tried to remember what the quotation was, another very clear phrase came into my head: 'in wrath remember mercy'. So I went on to pray this prayer too.

Now I realised that I was not praying for myself alone but interceding for the church and the world, especially our own little bit of the world, our own villages, and the churches round about us. We lived all the time with the rejection, indifference or hostility of the majority of the villagers. They were not only suspicious or contemptuous of the things that we did but their hearts were hardened against God. In both villages now we had visited them all, and most of them were deaf and blind to the gospel of our Lord Jesus Christ. This was not new. The people of Britain had been hardening their hearts against the God of their fathers for several generations. I was interceding for them: 'Enter not into judgement with your servants O Lord, for in your sight shall no man living be justified. In wrath remember mercy.'

The church was not much better. The Church of England was speeding down the road to financial ruin, but seemed to be blind to the unfaithfulness and corruption that infected its life. The smugness and complacency were incomprehensible, but apparently incorrigible. It was true that the Church of England tolerated us 'charismatics', but the bigger part of the church simply did not want to know what God was doing among us. I was interceding for the church too: 'Enter not into judgement with your servants, O Lord, for in your sight shall no man living be justified. In wrath remember mercy.'

As I got up from the floor, I felt dazed, not so much physically as spiritually dazed. The wrath of God was upon the church and the nation, but not because of their hardness of heart; his wrath was causing their hardness of heart. God had caused this hardening to come upon us, lest we should turn and be healed (Is 6:9-10). I had never understood such passages in the Bible, though I knew of many of them, and I was not sure I fully understood them now. But God was applying them for me to our generation, and revealing to me how to pray. He might yet be induced to relent, to repent of his wrath, to soften the hearts of the people that they might turn and be saved. So I continued to pray: 'In wrath remember mercy.'

My longing has been, and still is, to see the renewal of the church and the revival of the nation. People falling over, laughing, crying, roaring, shaking, is contemptible unless, in some mysterious way, it is part of that. But neither the church nor the nation will be changed except by people being changed, one by one. The only yardstick by which we can measure the 'Toronto Blessing', or any other activity of the church is this: is God being glorified and are lives being changed? The two things are inseparable in Christianity. God is glorified by changed lives, and he is not glorified by unchanged lives, whatever motions we go through. No less, lives are changed where God is glorified in spirit and truth; if lives are not being changed, God is not being glorified.

This yardstick needs to be applied across the board, not just to the 'Toronto Blessing'. The other things that people do in churches, the solemn processions in our cathedrals, the meetings of synods, the fund-raising events for the church roof: are they changing people's lives? If not, what is the point of it all? We had better close down.

Jesus came to redeem the world, which means change it. He came to lead people back to obedience to God, to reconcile them to God, to give them new hearts, new minds, new life. If we see that happening, it is Jesus; if we do not, it is not. I have seen lives being changed, not by me, but by the power of God: Ian and Gill, Peter and Margaret, John and Hazel, Dianne, Georgina, Richard and Ruby, Vera, Tim and Fiona, Brenda and Dave, Sarah-Jane, Simon, Steven and Andrew, Jan and Chris, Andrew, David, Lee, Mark, Daniel and Martin, Ivan and Lorraine, many more, and me. There are of course hundreds of other people in our villages whose lives have not been changed – or not yet. We are working on them, and I believe that God is too. 'Enter not into judgement with your servants, O Lord, for in your sight shall no man living be justified. In wrath remember mercy.'

If God uses somewhat drastic and bizarre methods to change people, what has that to do with me? Should I object or tell him to do it another way? We often need shaking, so let God shake us. We often need to be brought down, so let God knock us down. We often need to cry and everyone needs to laugh, so let's laugh and cry with God.

I am encouraged to read in Wesley's Journals that

these manifestations have happened before; indeed as one reads the small print of stories of revival it appears that they have often happened before. There seem to be seasons in the life of the church and the nation as there are seasons in nature. There is a cycle of harvesting, of which those of us who live in the countryside are perhaps more aware than those who live in the towns. The harvest is not continuous, all the year round; it comes only in its season.

Likewise, there seem to be spiritual seasons in the life of the church and the nation; it is not an annual cycle but one which covers perhaps 200 - 250 years. There is a season every so often when the fields are indeed white unto harvest, and the labourers go out and gather in souls, not by ones and twos but by hundreds and thousands. It seems to be in such seasons as these, seasons of revival, that the manifestations of the Spirit occur. The manifestations of the Spirit seem to appear like swallows, to announce that another summer of God's mercy and favour has come, that a season of harvesting is at hand. If that is true, then the reappearance of the manifestations of the Holy Spirit now, in such abundance, suggests that we are on the verge of a new revival. That is indeed our hope and prayer at St Nicholas' and St George's.

I have now been rector of these parishes for seven years. They have been seven years of sowing and growing, but not yet of great harvesting. Indeed they have been seven years of almost constant pruning. From the beginning, people have been leaving our two churches as well as joining them. We lost many of the traditionalists, and the half-hearted. We lost the occasional worshippers and the social conformists. As the churches and the services changed so we lost people at every step: we lost people when we introduced the new service book and the new songs; we lost people when we included the children in the Sunday morning services; we lost people when we introduced the gifts of the Spirit; we lost people again when we began to see the manifestations of the Spirit.

Jesus said, 'I am the true vine and my Father is the gardener. He cuts off every branch in me that bears no fruit, while every branch that does bear fruit he prunes, so that it will be even more fruitful' (Jn 15:1-2). It seems that pruning is to be expected in a church that is being made fruitful. Some months before the Toronto Blessing made a major impact on our churches, someone gave me a prophecy that the church was about to be pruned again. I did not want to know that at the time, but it proved to be true. It is ironical that the person who brought me the prophecy was one of the branches which itself was pruned away.

These seven years have not been lean years. God has constantly given us much more than he has taken away. But they have not been years of spectacular increase. I hope that the next seven years will be fat ones, years of abundance, of harvesting, even years of revival.

Lord I have heard of your fame;
     I stand in awe of your deeds, O Lord.
Renew them in our day,
     in our time make them known;
     in wrath remember mercy (Hab 3:2).

EPILOGUE

Six months after we had suspended the ministry of the Holy Spirit as an integral part of the Sunday morning service, we brought it back again. Some people still questioned whether this was the right place to do it: should it not be kept for less significant, more select occasions? I thought not. No one disputed that when we invited the Holy Spirit to come upon the congregation things happened. That was what had caused the trouble. Precisely for that reason, because God did things among us then which he did not do at other times, we needed to do it. How could I deprive God of this opportunity to touch his people; and how could I deprive the people of this opportunity to be touched by God?

Lord, come down on your people in increasing power. Amen.

I Will Pour Out My Spirit

by R. E. Davies

A comprehensive analysis of revivals past and present.

Many writers have tackled the theme of revival, but few have cast their nets so widely or so systematically. Dr Ron Davies looks at revivals in Scripture and throughout history, and also discerns key theological issues.

His topics include:
- Theological and biblical definitions
- The teaching of Jonathan Edwards, the classic theologian of revival
- A survey of major revivals of past and present
- Excesses and other problems accompanying revival
- Is possible for Christians to 'produce a revival' by prayer
- Can Christians by their actions bring revival to a premature end?
- What connection is there between revivals and the Second Coming?

'An excellent study. It fills a significant gap in the literature on revival.' – *James Bradley, Professor of Church History, Fuller Theological Seminary*

ISBN 1 85424 160 5   288pp large format   £9.99

To order this or any of the following books please contact your local bookshop, or in case of difficulty ring Monarch on 01892 652364, or write to: Monarch Publications, Broadway House, The Broadway, Crowborough, East Sussex TN6 1HQ.

Monarch
Publications

Speak To These Bones

by Martin Down

The wind of the Spirit blows through two traditional churches.

When Martin Down arrived with his wife Maureen to be interviewed for the position of Rector, the churchwarden asked anxiously, 'Will you change the services?' Neither he nor Martin expected that within a matter of months the Spirit would be changing a great deal more than the liturgy. When the miracles began, the people of Martin's parish started to realise that even in the most conservative churches, God is at work.

This is the humble, affectionate and wryly humorous account of a man willing to follow where God led. 'To try and run a church without the power from on high was like trying to run a car without petrol,' he comments. 'All the good ideas, new forms of worship, new songs – none of it is any use without the power of the Holy Spirit.'

'A sort of charismatic "Archers" – an extraordinary story of country folk.' – *Canon John Gunstone*

'Will give hope, encouragement and vision to all who read it.' – *Rev. Michael Mitton, Director, Anglican Renewal Ministries*

ISBN 1 85424 199 0   192pp small format   £3.99

Monarch Publications

Something Extraordinary Is Happening

by Andy and Jane Fitz-Gibbon
Foreword by John Arnott

'Each time Ken Gott prayed my body literally left the floor: I had never known such spiritual power… God has never been more real, more present and more available.'

At the turn of the century Sunderland witnessed a remarkable turning to Christ. People from all over the world came to experience for themselves the outpouring of the Holy Spirit. Contemporary accounts describe tears, healings and prostrate congregations.

Since the summer of 1994 similar events have occurred as literally tens of thousands of people have visited Sunderland Christian Centre. Lives have been changed, bodies and relationships healed, people have received a fresh power and vision from God for their ministries.

Andy and Jane Fitz-Gibbon are deeply involved in what is happening. In this first-hand account they describe the beginnings and ongoing development of this mighty movement of God. They record many instances of truly remarkable transformations in people attending the church. At all times they seek to preserve a balance and sensible approach despite their extraordinary material.

ISBN 1 85424 329 2   192pp small format   £4.99

Monarch
Publications

The Kiss Of Intimacy

by Andy and Jane Fitz-Gibbon

Ever since the Toronto Blessing swept across the church, wise commentators have been asking, 'Where are the fruit?' This profound and delightful book, which springs in part from the Sunderland experience of this time of refreshment, may be one such fruit.

The *Song of Songs* is a love poem, God's great affirmation of human sexuality. It is also a glorious picture of the relationship between God and his people, Christ and his Church. Dr Martyn Lloyd-Jones called it a 'mine of spiritual treasure'.

As Andy and Jane Fitz-Gibbon encountered the wave of spiritual refreshment, God seemed to be calling them to immerse themselves again in his love. 'The *Song* is to become your guide book, your resting place and the chamber of love where you will find me.'

'Full of profound and moving glimpses into the love of Christ for his bride… My prayer is that this book will lead many others into a deeper intimacy with the glorious Lover, crucified and risen, eternal and divine.' – *Rob Warner, author, speaker and pastor*

ISBN 1 85424 321 7   160pp small format   £4.99

Monarch
Publications

The Impact Of Toronto

Edited by Wallace Boulton
editor of *Renewal* magazine

The July 1994 issue of *Renewal* was at the printers when news reached the Renewal offices of extraordinary events unfolding at various London Churches. The Toronto Blessing had arrived in Britain.

Renewal has subsequently had the privilege of publishing a series of excellent articles on the whole phenomenon. Is this really of God? Is the long-prayed-for revival finally at hand? What about those who remain unaffected?

This volume brings together the very best of these pieces to provide a lasting record of what God has been doing in Britain and around the world. He is indeed 'making all things new'.

Includes contributions from: Michael Green, Eleanor Mumford, Nicky Gumbel, Terry Virgo, R. T. Kendall, Gerald Coates, Jane Grayshon and Peter Gammons.

ISBN 1 85424 315 2   128pp small format   £3.99

Monarch Publications